How to Pass

SECOND EDITION

NATIONAL 5

History

John A. Kerr and
Jerry Teale

HODDER
GIBSON
AN HACHETTE UK COMPANY

The Publishers would like to thank the following for permission to reproduce copyright material:

Photo credits

p.16 © National Museums of Scotland/Historic Environment Scotland; **p.27** © Hulton Archive/Getty Images; **p.33** © Private Collection/J. T. Vintage/Bridgeman Images; **p.40** © Mary Evans Picture Library; **p.49** © Mary Evans Picture Library; **p.62** © Hulton-Deutsch Collection/CORBIS/Corbis via Getty Images; **p.77** © Hulton Archive/Getty Images; **p.86** © Bettmann/Getty Images; **p.99** © CORBIS/Corbis via Getty Images; **p.110** © Harding Andrews, Emily J. (fl.1910)/Fawcett Library, London, UK/Bridgeman Images.

Every effort has been made to trace all copyright holders, but if any have been inadvertently overlooked the Publishers will be pleased to make the necessary arrangements at the first opportunity.

Although every effort has been made to ensure that website addresses are correct at time of going to press, Hodder Gibson cannot be held responsible for the content of any website mentioned in this book. It is sometimes possible to find a relocated web page by typing in the address of the home page for a website in the URL window of your browser.

Hachette UK's policy is to use papers that are natural, renewable and recyclable products and made from wood grown in sustainable forests. The logging and manufacturing processes are expected to conform to the environmental regulations of the country of origin.

Orders: please contact Bookpoint Ltd, 130 Park Drive, Milton Park, Abingdon, Oxon OX14 4SE. Telephone: (44) 01235 827720. Fax: (44) 01235 400454. Lines are open 9.00–5.00, Monday to Saturday, with a 24-hour message answering service. Visit our website at www.hoddereducation.co.uk. Hodder Gibson can also be contacted directly at hoddergibson@hodder.co.uk

© John A. Kerr and Jerry Teale 2018

First published in 2018 by
Hodder Gibson, an imprint of Hodder Education,
An Hachette UK Company
211 St Vincent Street
Glasgow G2 5QY

Impression number	5	4	3	2	1
Year	2022	2021	2020	2019	2018

Cover photo © I. Pilon/Shutterstock
Illustrations by Emma Golley at Redmoor Design and by Aptara, Inc.
Typeset in 13/15 Cronos Pro by Aptara, Inc.
Printed in Spain
A catalogue record for this title is available from the British Library
ISBN: 978 1 5104 2096 0

Contents

Introduction: How to revise

This revision book gives specific advice about eight of the most popular topics at National 5 History (see page 12), although the guidance on study skills and answering techniques applies to all topics. This book will help you to achieve your best possible result in the National 5 examination by telling you all you need to know about the exam and the tests you are likely to take.

It tells you **how** to learn, **what** to learn and provides lots of practice for the different types of questions you will answer. It even provides model answers and advice showing what makes a good answer and a weak answer.

By working your way through this book you will find it easier to understand and write assessment answers and, in the process, gather valuable extra information about course content.

You will also find advice about the assignment, a task you must do to complete the course successfully.

How to be a better learner

Before you start revising all the information you have to know for the exam, have you thought about how efficiently you learn? Do you spend hours just reading notes over and over again? Revise for a while then ask yourself some serious questions. How much of your revision can you really remember an hour after you have finished? How much can you remember the next day? How much can you remember the next week?

The following are just some examples of activities that will help you to revise for any subject, not just history.

But why bother doing different things?

Think about this:

If you always do what you have always done, then you will always get what you have always got.

If you *really* want to improve then things have to change. They will not change just because you want them to. By putting in the effort, you have the power to make a difference to yourself.

The pyramid of efficiency

This pyramid diagram shows on average what a person will remember 24 hours after a 'learning experience' if they do nothing to reinforce it. For example, if you sit and read over information and then do nothing to reinforce that reading then after 24 hours you will have forgotten 90 per cent of the information you read. That is not the best way to use your time.

After 24 hours you will remember...

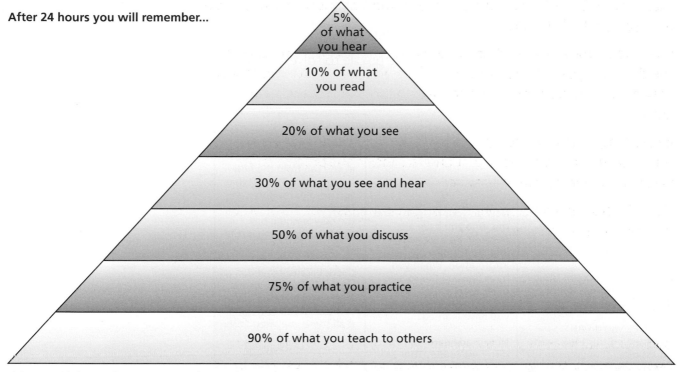

This pyramid shows what percentage of new information an average person would remember after 24 hours if they used the methods of learning shown here – AND if that person did nothing to reinforce the learning during the following 24 hours.

On the other hand, if you try to explain clearly what you have recently revised to a friend then you are using your learning for a purpose. That means you can expect to remember over 75 per cent of what you revised. The same is true if you just record your thoughts or information onto audio or video using your smartphone or tablet. So it makes sense to think about HOW you intend to learn.

The 'I really know this!' test

Think of a place you know really well. It could be a room in your house, a shop or a street or a quiet place you like.

From your memory, describe, list or draw in detail all the things you can see in your place. Try to be as detailed as you can, list things such as colours and patterns and where everything is in relation to everything else.

Next time you go to that place take your list with you. When you get there you will recognise instantly every single detail – but do those details appear on your list? I bet they don't.

Remember: The point is that recognising lots of detail is not the same as knowing it and being able to write it as a response to a question.

Now think about your revision. If you read over the same book or notes again and again you will feel you know it, but you are really just recognising your notes. Without the prompt of your notes in front of you, can you really be sure you know the information well enough to use it in an exam?

In the next few pages, you will find tips and ideas for making your revision more effective and maybe even more enjoyable.

How do you know what to revise?

Your brain works best when it has a definite puzzle to solve, so try these steps.

1

Decide on a focused topic or question from the section you have been studying.

BEFORE you do ANY revision on this topic, write a list of all that you already know about the subject. It might be quite a long list, but you only need to write it once. It shows you all the information that is in your long-term memory. So now you know what you **do not** have to revise – you already know it! And now you know what you **do** have to revise!

2

Now do your revision – and this time you have a purpose. You are now looking for **new** information. When you have finished this session of revision, write a new list of the new information you have learned.

Now shade each list in a different colour. That will make each list easier to see in your mind's eye.

3

A day after your revision, try to remember as much as you can from the new learning box. That is what you need to reinforce, so remember the colour of the new learning box and think what you wrote in it.

Check back to remind yourself what you wrote in the new learning box and then try to remember it all sometime later. Each time you do that you reinforce your new learning.

Stop and review

Here's another idea to help your learning.

1 When you have done no more than five minutes of revision STOP!
2 Write a heading in your own words which sums up the topic you have been revising.
3 Write a summary in no more than two sentences of what you have revised. Don't fool yourself. If you cannot do it, or do not want to do it, why not? Don't ever say to yourself, 'I know it, but I cannot put it into words'. That just means you don't know it well enough! So if you cannot write your summary, then revise that section again, knowing that you must write a summary at the end of it.

Your brain now knows exactly what it has to do. You will learn much more effectively.

We guarantee your revision will suddenly improve!

Use technology

Why should everything be written down?

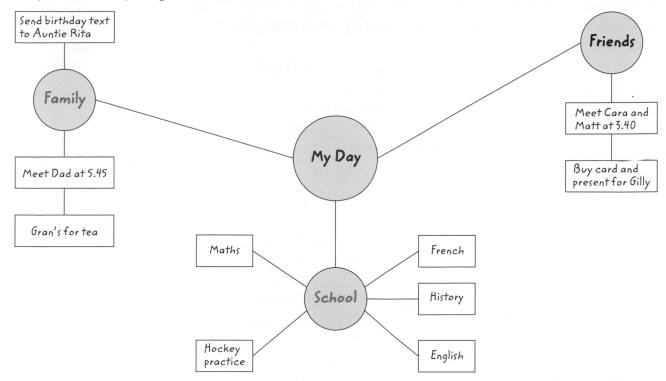

Have you thought about 'mental' maps, diagrams, cartoons and colour to help you learn? And rather than writing down notes, why not record your revision material?

What about having a text message revision session with friends?

Why not make a video diary where you tell the camera what you are doing, what you think you have learned and what you still have to do?

You could share these things with your friends. Keep in touch with your friends about how and what they are revising through Facebook or other social media sites.

They deserve a laugh. Nobody said revision had to be boring. And after you gain the results you want you can watch the videos again and wonder why you got so stressed in the first place!

Use games

Word search

Here is how to do an effective word search game:
- Work together with a group of friends. There are lots of apps that allow you to make word search puzzles on tablets or phones.
- Design a word search about ten squares by ten squares. It's your choice but keep it realistic.
- Your puzzle must only contain facts linked to the topic you are revising. You can do others which, for example, focus on ideas, names or vocabulary.
- The words or phrases can go in any direction and phrases can be split.
- You must write in all the names and words and phrases you want to use in your own word search.

- Fill up empty squares with random letters.
- Remember to keep a note of where your answers are but do not show your friends.
- Give each of your word searches a title, based on the topic all your words and names are linked to.
- Beneath your word search DO NOT list the answers. Instead, write helpful clues or definitions to assist your partner in finding the correct answers.
- When you have completed your puzzle, swap it for your friend's word search and use the clues to the puzzle you received to find the answers.
- Meanwhile your friend can be solving your puzzle.

Why do this game?
- By doing the word search, you must know or find out detailed information.
- You must know how to spell your information.
- You must know what the information means exactly before you can write your definition or clue.
- You must know more information to solve your partner's word search.

All this time your brain is active and not passive, just hoping to 'memorise'.

Hangman

Here is how to do a hangman game:
- Design the usual hangman scene with steps and gallows.
- Decide with your friend what topic all the names and words you use will be about.
- Draw the blank space dashes accurately and remember to make sure your spelling is correct.
- Your friend starts to guess a correct letter. As soon as the first letter is written, your friend's brain is sorting out all the relevant facts and names containing that letter. This game also helps you to learn the spelling of difficult names and words.
- When the game is completed do another.

Make electronic files

Many of you will use notebooks full of blue or black ink writing. Many of the pages will not be especially attractive or memorable. But it's making material memorable that is most important.

Most people have access to a computer or tablet. **Use it to help you.**

- Start by opening up a new file for each topic you are revising, for example, 'What the Western Front was like for Scottish soldiers in the First World War'.
- Then you could start by summarising your class notes. Your typing might be slow but it will get faster and typing avoids any poor handwriting concerns.
- Next you can add different fonts and colours to make your work stand out. But the **most important** thing is that you can easily paste in relevant pictures, cartoons and diagrams to make your work more attractive and MEMORABLE.

If you don't know how to find images, use Google images and make your choice. By doing so you are immediately using your brain to search for relevant items to your topic and that requires you to use your understanding. Ask your friends if you're not sure how to do those things. Trade with them some of the advice from this book!

Story boards

Everyone can draw stick people and many people are really good sketchers.

Many people are also visual learners, so putting a story into pictures can really help you to remember information. Choose a part of your course to revise and think how you could simplify it into a set of cartoon scenes that tell the main story.

Race relations in the USA in the 1950s

Segregation of black and white students into black and white schools

The Supreme Court decision in 1954 ended segregation in schools. Civil rights campaigners celebrate

Soldiers protect the children going to school in Little Rock, Arkansas in 1957

Pictures or words

There is a lot of advice given here in words. But the ideas map below shows many different ideas on how to make your revision more effective and enjoyable.

To make you really think about the ideas on the map draw it yourself.

Add colour, perhaps colour-coding revision methods that you **have** tried, **will** try and **might** try and also those you really do not want to do.

Then add as many new ideas about how to revise as you can. Once again you are forcing your brain to be active. Try to add as many new ideas to the map as possible.

There are better ways to improve your learning.

Part One: How you will be tested

Chapter 1
The assignment

Now that you have some ideas about how to revise, it's time to move on to thinking about how to get the best marks possible for the exam.

Put simply, there are **two** parts to the National 5 examination:

- The **first** part of your exam is the assignment, which you will probably complete during the spring term before you sit your exam.
- The **second** part is the exam, which you will sit in May. Much more on that later!

What is the assignment?

The assignment is an essay written under exam conditions and then sent to the SQA to be marked.

Why do I have to do an assignment?

It's a chance to show off what you can do! You have very limited time in the final exam and examiners know that answers written under exam pressure are not likely to show the best of you. The assignment gives you the chance to write the best essay you can.

Why is the assignment so important?

It's really important to do as well as you can in the assignment, as the mark you get is part of your final National 5 award total. In fact, the assignment counts for 20 marks out of a total of 100, so doing well in the assignment can provide you with a very useful launch pad for future success.

How long does my essay have to be?

The answer's simple – as much as you can write in one hour! There are *no* word limits in the assignment. Most people can write about one page of A4 in fifteen minutes, so it is possible to write an essay that is about four pages long.

Should I try to choose a title that's fresh and new and different?

You don't have to. Some candidates make life difficult for themselves by making up hard titles for their essay. Ask your teacher or tutor if you're unsure. It's not necessary to invent a completely new title.

Remember: KISS

Keep
It
Simple,
Stupid

You are allowed to research a local history topic if you want to. However, it's very unlikely that your essay will be marked by someone who knows your local area, so you could be putting yourself at a disadvantage. It would be safer to choose something from the history you have already been studying. This should give you a head start.

Avoid doing something risky – you only get one chance at this assignment.

Are there types of questions to avoid?

Yes.

Firstly, it makes sense to choose a question from the course topics you are studying. You can check this at: www.sqa.org.uk

Secondly, your essay title should be based on a question that allows you to use your evidence to answer the question. Titles such as *'To what extent was the Scots' victory at Stirling Bridge due to the leadership of William Wallace?'* are good.

On the other hand, try to avoid titles that are just statements. Essays with headings such as *'The Slave Trade'*, *'The Crusades'*, or *'Appeasement'* are very likely to fail because the marker has no way of knowing what you are trying to do apart from write a description of the subject in the title. A good way to make sure your essay is issue based is to include words such as *'To what extent'* or *'How important'* in the title – for example *'How important was the Rowntree report as a reason for the Liberal Reforms 1906–1914?'*

Finally, try **not** to make up questions that are too complicated or that ask two questions within the same title. A useful tip is to see if you have used the word *'and'* in the title. If you have then you might have made up two questions. An example of a double question is, *'How important was Hitler in getting the Nazis to power and then keeping them in power?'* That's bad enough, but think of the work involved in writing this essay, done by a student some years ago – *'How important was the Act of Union, who was against it and why, and who was for it and why?'*!

Remember, you are in charge of choosing your questions so why make life difficult for yourself?

What if my assignment title appears in the final exam?

You just got lucky!

If you choose your assignment from 'mainstream titles' it is quite possible that your topic, and perhaps even a title similar to your assignment, will appear in the final exam. There is **no** restriction about answering that question using the memory you have of doing the assignment. But be careful to adapt your information to fit the exact question asked in the exam.

What is the resource sheet?

This is a piece of A4 paper that you take with you when you go to write up your assignment. You are allowed to write no more than 200 words on the resource sheet. The resource sheet should contain the quotes from sources you intend to use along with the author of the source and the title of the source you used. It can also contain a plan for what you intend to write including bullet points and lists of information. The only thing it must **not** have is parts of your assignment already written out for you to copy. This will show the person at SQA who marks your assignment, that you have researched, selected and organised information.

How should I write and use my resource sheet?

During your research you will record and organise information which helps to address the question you have chosen. You should then use your resource sheet to bring together the sources and evidence you want to use in your essay.

Will my resource sheet be marked?

You will not be given a mark for your completed resource sheet but it may help the marker to get a clearer picture of what you are trying to do in your essay. There is no time limit for completing your sheet and no word count. The purpose of the resource sheet is to support you when you come to write up the findings of your research in your essay.

The resource sheet is YOURS. You can change it, colour it or print it out. You can write it anywhere, anytime before you write your assignment under exam conditions.

How should I begin my assignment?

It is sometimes hard to start writing if you have not thought through your answer so be prepared and use your introduction to your advantage. You should write an outline of your introduction on your resource sheet. That will get you started and give you a chance to outline the main parts of the essay that you will develop later. As you write the later parts of your essay, you could refer back to your introduction as a guide to help you remember what to write about next.

How should I write the middle part of my assignment?

Outline each paragraph you are intending to write on your resource sheet so you can use this to keep your essay focused on the question. You should aim to write a main starting sentence to begin each paragraph.

It is essential that you give a balanced answer. The point of your essay might be to show that your research leads you to conclude that one factor was particularly important in causing an event or development to take place. For example, you might argue that Martin Luther King played a very important role in the success of the civil rights movement. To balance your answer you would have to show that you understand there were other factors in this success even though you consider them to be less important. For example, the students in the South who organised successful sit-in protests at lunch counters.

Remember: you should use supporting evidence throughout your essay. History skills should run through the essay. You must make good use of the sources that you have included on your resource sheet. Make reference if you can to the reliability and accuracy of the sources you have used.

It is also helpful to remind yourself to include mini conclusions linking each paragraph back to the main title, so you keep your arguments going and don't fall back into story telling with little connection to the main question.

How should I organise my conclusion?

You must have a strong conclusion which answers the question you set yourself. Summarise the factors which you have identified and explain which factor you think is most important, giving a reason for your choice. You must prepare your conclusion carefully. You could write a summary on your resource sheet.

And remember – try to ensure your conclusion ends on a high note, perhaps with an appropriate quote that provides an overall answer to the question that supports your main argument.

What do I have to do in the exam?

The question paper is made up of three sections:

Section 1: Scottish contexts

Section 2: British contexts

Section 3: European and World contexts

In each section you will select one **part** to answer questions on:

Section 1: Scottish contexts

Part A: The Wars of Independence, 1286–1328

Part B: Mary Queen of Scots and the Scottish Reformation, 1542–1587

Part C: The Treaty of Union, 1689–1715

Part D: Migration and Empire, 1830–1939

Part E: The Era of the Great War, 1900–1928

Section 2: British contexts

Part A: The Creation of the Medieval Kingdoms, 1066–1406

Part B: War of the Three Kingdoms, 1603–1651

Part C: The Atlantic Slave Trade, 1770–1807

Part D: Changing Britain, 1760–1914

Part E: The Making of Modern Britain, 1880–1951

Section 3: European and World contexts

Part A: The Cross and the Crescent, the Crusades 1071–1192

Part B: 'Tea and Freedom', the American Revolution 1774–1783

Part C: USA 1850–1880

Part D: Hitler and Nazi Germany, 1919–1939

Part E: Red Flag: Lenin and the Russian Revolution, 1894–1921

Part F: Mussolini and Fascist Italy, 1919–1939

Part G: Free at Last? Civil Rights in the USA, 1918–1968

Part H: Appeasement and the Road to War, 1918–1939

Part I: World War II, 1939–1945

Part J: The Cold War 1945–1989

So to summarise, you must answer questions on three parts, one part taken from each of the three sections listed above.

Hints & tips

Timing is important. Make sure you have a watch or a clock so that you have some way of telling how much time you have left.

You have two hours and 20 minutes to answer the questions on the three sections you have studied. That gives you just over 45 minutes to answer each section.

You will answer 14 questions, divided into sections of 5, 5 and 4. The section with 4 questions will be rotated randomly. But be careful! – Allow yourself about 1 minute to read and think about each question.

Also, be aware that some questions are worth more marks than others, so give yourself a little more time to answer these questions than for the questions with lower marks. For example, in two of the sections there will be a 9 mark question. You only need to make 5 points to answer this question and you can gain extra marks for setting out your answer correctly in paragraphs, with an introduction and conclusion.

5

Answering the exam questions

The first rule is simple and is the most important thing that will get you marks.

Answer the question that you are asked, NOT what you would like it to ask.

The exam paper has six types of questions:

Type 1: the **describe** question

Type 2: the **explain** question

Type 3: the **to what extent**, **how important** or **how successful** question

Type 4: the **evaluate the usefulness** question

Type 5: the **compare** question

Type 6: the **how fully** question

1. The 'describe' question (4 marks)

In this type of question you must:

- describe what happened or
- describe the effects of an event or development
- include four pieces of your own knowledge, known as **recall** (there is no source to help you with information so your answer will be based on your own recall)
- use recall that is relevant to the question
- use recall that is correct and accurate.

You can always gain an extra mark for adding relevant detail to back up the point you are making.

Example

Question

Describe the effects of the introduction of conscription during the First World War. (4 marks)

You need to make **four** separate points from recall. You could mention that:

- all men between the ages of 19 and 40 could be called up
- married men and men up to the age of 50 were later included
- the physically or mentally unfit could claim exemption
- some men doing work of national importance were exempted (that means they did not have to join the army, for example, coal miners)
- men who ran businesses that were directly linked to helping the war effort were exempted
- men could claim exemption on grounds of their conscience
- tribunals were set up to hear the cases of men seeking exemption
- tribunals always included one military representative and exemption was rarely granted
- the National Conscription Fellowship (NCF) was set up
- conscientious objectors were often treated very harshly and had a difficult time in prison.

You can always gain an extra mark if you bring in more information to back up the point you are making.

For example: *One effect was that all men between the ages of 19 and 40 could be called up* (1 mark). *If you were conscripted you could make an appeal to be excused service which would go to a local military tribunal* (1 extra mark).

2. The 'explain' question (6 marks)

To be successful with this type of question you must:

- give six reasons why something happened. These must be genuine reasons relevant to the question and not just a collection of facts with no attempt to explain why they are linked to the question
- use recall that is relevant to the question (once again, there is no source to help you)
- use recall that is correct and accurate.

You can always gain an extra mark for adding relevant detail to back up the point you are making.

Hints & tips ⭐

Don't steal time!
Aim to complete all your answers in about seven minutes. Do not write for longer than that or you will be stealing time from your other answers.

Example

Question

Explain the reasons why many people emigrated from Ireland in the nineteenth century. (6 marks)

You need to make **six** separate points from recall. You could mention:

- Ireland's growing population at this time
- that lack of industry in Ireland led to unemployment
- the decline in craft industries
- that landlords were evicting some of their tenants
- that landlords were increasing rents
- that a family's land was often divided up between the children, leading to smaller plots
- inadequate diet, the people relied on potatoes
- that the potato famine forced many to flee from Ireland.

You can always gain an extra mark for adding relevant detail to back up the point you are making. For example: *People emigrated from Ireland in the 19th century because of Ireland's growing population at this time* (1 mark). *This meant there were many more mouths to feed when food was short* (1 extra mark).

3. The 'to what extent', 'how important' or 'how successful' question (9 marks)

To be successful with this type of question you must:

- write a short introduction showing that you understand that other factors have to be considered apart from the one mentioned in the question
- decide how important the factor mentioned in the question was in explaining why something happened
- identify other factors which might explain why this happened
- include at least five pieces of relevant information
- use your own judgement to give a short conclusion which sums up your answer to the question
- give a reason to support your conclusion.

Hints & tips

Organise your information into a balanced answer, such as writing:
*'**Yes, the case of the Zong was important** ... **However there were other reasons** for the growth of the abolitionist cause, such as ...'*

Example ⚑

Question

How important was the case of the Zong to the growth of the abolitionist campaign? (9 marks)

Write a short introduction showing that you understand there were other factors which contributed to the growth of abolitionism. List these factors in your introduction.

For example:

The case of the Zong was important to the growth of the abolitionist campaign, but there were other factors such as the contributions of Wilberforce, Clarkson and Equiano.

Now take a new paragraph and make at least two points to explain why the Zong was important.

You could mention:

- how the case of the Zong highlighted the cruelty of the slave trade
- that abolitionists publicised the details of the case
- that the court case was widely reported in newspapers.

You should then balance your answer by giving other reasons for the growth of the campaign, such as:

- the parliamentary campaign led by Wilberforce
- Thomas Clarkson toured Britain giving lectures
- the many churchmen who preached about the cruelty of the trade
- the testimony of freed slaves like Olaudah Equiano.

You should finish with a conclusion that gives an overall answer to the question and support it with a reason for the judgement you have made.

For example: *Overall, the case was a very important reason for the growth of the movement because it showed so many people how cruel the slave trade was.*

4. The 'evaluate the usefulness' question (5 marks)

It might be helpful to base your answer around the following guide questions:

- **WHO** produced the source? Why is the *authorship* of the source relevant and therefore useful in assessing the value of a source?
- **WHEN** was the source produced and how might that help in the evaluation of the source?
- **WHY** was the source produced? What did the person who produced the source want the readers to think or do or feel because of the information in the source? You must also state why each of the points you are writing about makes the source useful as evidence in terms of the question.

You can get up to four marks for commenting on these aspects.

You should then ask:

- **WHAT** information is in the source and how relevant is that to the question?
- **WHAT'S NOT THERE?** What important information is missing from the source that makes you think the source is not as useful as it could be?

You can get a maximum of two marks for each of these. Remember, to get the mark, you must include an evaluative comment with each point you make i.e. *the source is useful because...* or *the source is less useful because...*

Hints & tips ★

*In the type of question shown in the example below, it is never enough just to **describe** what is in a source.*

Evaluate means to judge how good a source is as evidence for finding out about something. The short answer is that it will always be partly useful, but that it will never be entirely useful in giving all the information you need.

Watch out for distractors. The sources will contain points which are not relevant to the question asked. Leave these out of your answer.

Example

Question

Evaluate the usefulness of Source A as evidence about the impact of poverty on British people at the turn of the century. (5 marks)

Source A is from the autobiography of Faith Osgerby, who grew up in Yorkshire at the beginning of the twentieth century.

> My father was a stone mason but also kept cows for his milk round. My mother had a great deal to put up with. Seven young children to clothe and feed and little money to do it. Also my elder sister was an invalid after having polio as a baby. Doctors had to be paid for their services and I remember two doctors coming to the house to operate on her legs and feet.

You need to make **five** clear points about the usefulness of the source.

You would probably start by arguing that the source does provide useful evidence about the impact of poverty.

You should comment on who wrote the source, when it was written and why it was written. You must also make clear why each piece of information you are commenting is useful in terms of the question. You could mention:

- the source was written by someone who had lived through poverty
- the source is an autobiography written by someone who lived in Britain at the beginning of the twentieth century
- it was written to explain what it was like to live in poverty.

You should also comment on what the source says:

- the source tells us that the author's father did two jobs
- it mentions that having seven young children made things more difficult
- it mentions that medical care had to be paid for.

However, you could decide that in some ways the source is not very useful because of important information that has not been mentioned.

- the source doesn't mention the lack of support for the poor
- it doesn't mention the impact of poverty on old people
- it doesn't deal with unemployment, which could place a family in greater poverty.

5. The 'compare' question (4 marks)

To be successful with this type of question you must:

- make clear connections between the two sources but do not just describe them
- avoid only writing 'Source A says...' and then 'Source B says...'; you will not get marks for that
- explain the point you are making by using your own words and then use the sources to support your point
- repeat this again to make **two** full comparisons. It is also possible to get 4 marks by identifying 4 separate points of disagreement or agreement and explaining what the agreement or disagreement is about in each case.

Hints & tips

You will always get two questions that ask you to compare two sources in your exam. One of the questions will have two sources that agree with each other. The other question will contain sources that disagree.

Example

Question

Compare the views in Sources A and B as evidence about the reasons for the Bolshevik success in October 1917. (4 marks)

Sources A and **B** discuss the reasons for the success of the October Revolution in 1917.

Source A

It was very clear that despite what they said, the Bolsheviks did not have the support of Russian people. The October Revolution was not inevitable. The Bolsheviks simply grabbed an opportunity to seize power for themselves. This was only possible because of the chaos caused by the First World War. The revolution was a skilfully led military operation involving only a handful of people.

Source B

In the months leading up to the Revolution the Bolsheviks won massive support among the workers and peasants of Russia. This was because the Bolsheviks demanded 'Peace, Bread and Land'. The October Revolution was the result of a great uprising of the downtrodden Russian people. The Bolsheviks simply guided those who had revolted because they had had enough of their misery and wanted a better life.

For this type of question you must say whether you think the sources agree or not and state what they agree about.

If you make simple comparisons like this then you will need four simple comparisons to get full marks. If you support your simple comparison with evidence from the sources, that is called a developed comparison. Two developed comparisons are worth the full 4 marks.

For this specific question you would probably decide that the two sources disagree. You could then back this up with two of the following comparisons:

- Source A says that the Bolsheviks did not have the support of the Russian people but Source B says they had massive support
- Source A says that the revolution was caused by the chaos of war but Source B says it was brought about by people who had had enough of misery and wanted a better life
- Source A says the Bolsheviks led the revolution but Source B says they simply guided it.

Here is a sample comparison that would get good marks. Try it yourself.

Source A and B disagree about the reasons for the success of the October Revolution.

Firstly, they disagree about the support from the Russian people. Source A does not think the Bolsheviks had much support. It states, 'It was very clear that despite what they said the Bolsheviks did not have the support of Russian people'. However, Source B thinks they had massive support and states, 'the Bolsheviks won massive support among the workers and peasants of Russia'.

Now use this technique for at least ONE other comparison.

6. The 'how fully' question (6 marks)

To be successful with this type of question you must:

- start your answer by showing that you understand that the source does not fully explain the issue
- select information from the source which is relevant to the question – usually there will be three points of information in the source for you to use
- use recall that is accurate and relevant to make your answer more balanced.

Example

Question

How fully does Source A describe the improvements which led to better health in Britain's cities in the nineteenth century? (6 marks)

Source A describes improvements that led to improved health in British cities during the nineteenth century.

> People living in Britain's cities at the beginning of the nineteenth century suffered terrible living conditions. There were a number of changes that brought about improvements in health during the century. These included the control and then the steady reduction of lethal diseases of childhood. This was achieved by improvement of the urban environment through the provision of cleaner water and better sewerage. The efforts of doctors, nurses and midwives were also beginning to be felt in working-class communities.

You should introduce your answer by saying that Source A describes improvements fairly well...but not fully.

You should then support this by pointing out that the source mentions:

- the control of lethal diseases of childhood
- improved water/sewerage
- the efforts of doctors, nurses and midwives.

You should then say that the source does not give an entirely full description of health improvements because important information is left out such as

- Victorian hospital building programs in Scottish cities
- Local Government Act led to the appointment of Medical Officers
- slum clearance
- local authorities providing better washing facilities
- local authorities controlling overcrowding in houses.

Part Two: What you must know

Now that you know HOW to answer the questions, all you have to do is to be sure of the subject content.

You should have notes and books to provide you with all the detailed content you need, so the next section of this book will only provide content outlines. Please note that there are twenty possible topics (five in Section 1, five in Section 2 and ten in Section 3), but due to space limitations this book concentrates on the eight most popular topics.

The eight most popular topics are:

Scottish contexts:

Chapter 3: Migration and Empire, 1830–1939

Chapter 4: The Era of the Great War, 1900–1928

British contexts:

Chapter 5: The Atlantic Slave Trade, 1770–1807

Chapter 6: Changing Britain, 1760–1914

Chapter 7: The Making of Modern Britain, 1880–1951

European and World contexts:

Chapter 8: Hitler and Nazi Germany, 1919–1939

Chapter 9: Red Flag: Lenin and the Russian Revolution, 1894–1921

Chapter 10: Free at Last? Civil Rights in the USA, 1918–1968

After each content guide that follows there will also be examples of questions and outline answers. (You will find advice on how to answer each type of question, as well as comments on what makes a good or weak answer, in Part 1 of this book.)

The outline answers in this section have three purposes:

1 They provide an outline of what you should have in your answer.
   - You can choose to look closely at the outline before you write an answer.
2 You can write an answer to the question and use the outline answer here as a self check list.
   - Ask yourself if you have all the information here and if you have structured your answer correctly.
   - You will also get some help by looking at model answers later in this book.
3 The outline answers also provide more information on the topic.

Chapter 3

Migration and Empire, 1830–1939

Immigration to Scotland, 1830s–1939

The first part of the syllabus is about immigration to Scotland between the 1830s and 1939.

What you should know

To be successful in this section you must be able to:

★ explain why different groups of immigrants decided to settle in Scotland
★ describe where different groups of immigrants settled in Scotland.

Between the 1830s and the 1930s Scotland became home to immigrants from various parts of the world. The four largest groups to settle in Scotland during this period were Irish, Jews, Lithuanians and Italians.

Why did these four groups of people settle in Scotland?

Irish

Most Irish came to Scotland to escape poverty, unemployment and hunger. In the 1840s a disease destroyed the potato crop, year after year. In total about two million emigrated to escape the famine.

Irish immigrants in Scotland often settled in the west of Scotland, around Glasgow. There were thousands of jobs in the new growing industries such as cotton factories, coal mines, ironworks and building the railway network.

Other Scottish cities also attracted Irish migrants. Living and working conditions in the industrial cities and factories of Scotland were hard but better than what they had left behind in Ireland.

Jews

Large numbers of Jews arrived in Scotland between 1880 and 1914. Most were poor and came from Russia and Poland.

Many Jews migrated to escape pogroms back in their home countries. A pogrom was an attack on Jews often organised by the local authorities to make Jews leave the area.

Many Jews also migrated because they were not able to become skilled craftsmen or professional people in their home countries because of prejudice and religious persecution.

Key words

Emigrant – someone who decides to leave their home country and settle somewhere else.

Immigrant – someone who arrives in a new country intending to settle there.

Migrate – to move from one country to another.

Pogrom – an organised attack on Jews, usually in Russia or Poland.

By the late nineteenth century travel became cheaper and faster so many people took the opportunity to migrate.

Lithuanians

Lithuanians emigrated in large numbers between the 1860s and 1914. About 7000 settled in Scotland. Lithuanians moved because taxes were very high in their home country and income from farming had fallen. Another reason why many farmers moved was because the population was increasing and good farming land became scarce.

Many Lithuanians settled in Lanarkshire and Ayrshire and took jobs in the coal, iron and steel industries.

Italians

Italians settled in Scotland in large numbers after 1880. By 1914 there were 4500 Italians in Scotland but unlike other immigrant groups, Italians settled all over Scotland.

At first the Italians who sold ice cream, and even fish and chips, worked from barrows, which they pushed along streets. Soon however, hard working Italian families opened up shops and cafés.

Some Scots complained that Italian cafés opened on a Sunday. This offended some strict Protestants. They also complained that Italian cafés opened late in the evening and that the shops attracted groups of youngsters.

Other Scots liked the Italian cafés because they did not sell alcohol and provided a place for youngsters to meet up with their friends.

What was the impact of immigration on Scotland? Did Scotland benefit from its links with the Empire?

The British Empire helped to make the Scottish economy very strong. For example, the shipbuilding industry, especially around Glasgow, benefitted from the demand for shipping to carry on trade.

The Empire provided raw materials for Scottish industries such as sugar and tobacco. In turn, Scotland then sold its products to the Empire, usually transported on ships built in Scotland or packed in jute sacks made in Scotland.

Many Scots found jobs and built up businesses in the Empire and many then invested their profits in their home country. For example, money made in the jute industry was used by wealthy merchants to buy and improve Scottish rural estates or to build large mansions in the suburbs of towns such as Broughty Ferry.

However, by the 1930s the balance of trade had shifted. Scotland now faced competition from industries that had grown up in the Empire, such as Indian factories that could produce jute products for a lower cost than businesses in Scotland. Scotland had lost its advantage.

> **Time to reflect !**
>
> Try to find somewhere in your family tree where you have an ancestor who migrated to Scotland. As a Scot, you probably do! Is there anything in your life that keeps up the traditions and culture of your immigrant ancestors? You might take it for granted but think about it.

The immigrant experience in Scotland, 1830s–1939

The second part of the syllabus is about the experience of immigrants to Scotland between the 1830s and 1939.

What you should know

To be successful in this section you must be able to:
* ★ describe the living conditions and jobs of immigrants
* ★ explain why there were tensions between Scots and immigrants
* ★ describe how some groups integrated more easily than others.

Key words

Assimilate – to mix in with the local population.
Discrimination – treating people differently, usually in an unfair way.
Sectarian – divisions between groups of people which are based on different religions.

How easily did different groups of immigrants to Scotland manage to assimilate?

Irish

Irish immigrants were poor and could only afford to live in the cheapest and poorest areas of the industrial towns of central Scotland. Many Scots resented the Irish immigrants because they increased the demand for housing and jobs, which meant rents were kept high and wages were kept low.

Religion was also an issue. Many of the Irish immigrants were Catholic and priests worked hard to provide education and help for the new families settling in Scotland. The Church also provided social and sporting clubs where Irish immigrants could relax and keep alive their religious and cultural habits from 'the old country'.

The mainly Protestant Scots were suspicious of the immigrants, who kept themselves to themselves. Some claimed that Protestant identity was being threatened by Catholic immigration. They began the Orange Lodge organisation. Football clubs were examples of the sectarian divide in Scotland, with Catholic Celtic facing Protestant Rangers in Glasgow and Hibernian and Hearts in Edinburgh displaying the same split in the population.

Between 1830 and 1930, anti-Irish and anti-Catholic feelings were stirred up in newspapers and books which claimed that the Irish were 'an inferior race'.

For many years, the Irish faced discrimination in employment because they were Catholic, but as the years went by Scots and Irish intermarried and many Scots today have Irish ancestors.

Protestant Irish usually mixed well with the local Scots. They shared the same religion, culture and language. Protestant Irish found it fairly easy to get skilled jobs in shipbuilding and engineering, jobs that were blocked to the Catholic Irish.

Jews

Jews were unlikely to assimilate into Scottish culture because of their religious and cultural differences and often kept to themselves. Some Jews faced anti-Semitism, which means they were discriminated against because they were Jewish.

Jews worked in jobs that did not directly threaten Scottish workers. Many Jews worked in cigarette factories and others became tailors in Glasgow. Wealthier Jews provided some financial help to the poorer Jewish immigrants from eastern Europe in the late nineteenth century. In summary, the Jewish community tended to look after each other.

Lithuanians

At first Lithuanians were unpopular as Scottish miners saw the immigrants as a threat to their jobs. Lithuanians were used as strike breakers, working while Scottish miners were on strike for better wages. Eventually, the leaders and the newspapers of the Lithuanian community organised the Lithuanian workers to support Scottish workers.

Lithuanians were also Catholic and faced some anti-Catholic prejudice.

It's more difficult to establish how much Lithuanians mixed with the Scottish communities in the past because many Lithuanians simply changed their surnames to local sounding names.

Lithuanian and Scottish workers at a brickworks at Carfin, Lanarkshire, c.1910–20.

Italians

Italians did not make a great effort to mix with the Scottish communities because many saw living in Scotland as a temporary situation and intended to return home in a few years.

Italian immigrants kept themselves to themselves and often intermarried and worked within family businesses.

Italians tended to be treated well in Scotland since they provided popular fast foods. In the 1930s, when Mussolini (the leader of Italy) became a supporter and friend of Hitler and Europe drifted towards war, some hostility to Italians began to appear.

Did immigrants have a political impact on Scotland?

The answer to this is yes. Until the early twentieth century most Irish Catholics voted for the Liberal Party. After the Liberal government executed the leaders of the Easter Rising of 1916 in Dublin, many Irish Catholics in Scotland moved their support to the Labour Party. This was a major reason for the rise of the Labour Party in Scotland.

Conversely, many Protestant Irish immigrants voted for the Conservative/Unionist Party because they wanted Ireland to remain part of the UK.

Lithuanian and Jewish immigrants became politically active in two ways. One was to join a trade union and campaign for better working conditions. In this way, immigrants and local workers began to integrate more. The second route into political action was to vote for and work within the Independent Labour Party, campaigning for better living conditions and political reform.

Italian immigrants were less influential in politics as many of them were concerned only with earning enough money to return to Italy. In the 1920s, some Italian immigrants were associated with Mussolini's Fascist Party and there were some scuffles in Scottish cities as tension grew between Italy and the UK in the 1930s.

Time to reflect

Nowadays there are many eastern European people living in Scotland. Do you welcome them, dislike them or just take no notice? How might your feelings be affected by where you live and what your job prospects are? Are you being fair or does fairness not matter?

Scottish emigration, 1830s–1939

The third part of the syllabus is about Scottish emigration between the 1830s and 1939.

Key words

Missionaries – people who travel abroad with the intention of persuading people to become Christians.

Technological changes – new machines were invented to speed up production but often meant fewer workers were needed.

What you should know

To be successful in this section you must be able to:

★ explain what is meant by 'push' and 'pull' reasons for emigration
★ explain why people emigrated from Scotland
★ describe the areas to which Scots migrated
★ explain why people emigrated from the Scottish Lowlands.

Why did Scots leave Scotland?

'Push' and 'pull'

Between 1830 and 1930, it has been estimated that over two million people left Scotland, either for 'push' reasons or 'pull' reasons.

Push reasons mean that Scots were **forced** to move, either as a result of losing their jobs or their homes. In the Highlands, 'push' reasons included eviction to make way for more profitable sheep farms or later to make way for tourism. In the Lowlands, unemployment in factory towns and technological changes in farming all pushed people into thinking about emigration.

A pull reason is something that **attracts**. These 'pull' reasons included incentives such as promises of cheap land, paid for travelling expenses and the hope of a better life somewhere else! Scots were also persuaded to emigrate by emigration societies and government schemes that helped people move and even by the desire to do missionary work overseas.

Highland Clearances

During the nineteenth century Highland landlords changed their style of farming. The Clearances meant that the old farming system was replaced by sheep farming. That meant large areas were used only for sheep grazing. Surplus tenants were 'cleared' off the Highland estates. These clearances continued throughout most of the nineteenth century.

Over-population was also a problem in the Highlands. There were too many people trying to make a living on too little fertile land.

The potato blight, a disease that destroyed potatoes, affected the Highlands as well as Ireland. Some landowners built new villages, such as Ullapool, on the coast for their homeless tenants but many Highlanders chose emigration as the answer to their problems.

Missionaries

In the early nineteenth century, Christian missionary expeditions went out to 'darkest Africa' to convert the natives to Christianity. By the late nineteenth century Scottish Christian missions were so successful in Africa that they set the example for other nations to copy. The most famous missionaries, who inspired other Scots to migrate and set up schools, hospitals and missions, were Mungo Park, David Livingstone and Mary Slessor.

Emigration societies and government schemes

In the 1850s, the Highland and Island Emigration Society raised money to help people who were suffering during the potato famine. It helped send emigrants to Australia.

The British and Canadian governments also started the Crofter Colonisation Scheme, which was intended to help people migrate from Scotland and settle on the Canadian prairies.

By the later nineteenth century emigration had increased, partly as a result of shorter travelling times across the Atlantic to the USA and Canada. Travelling time was an important concern to workers who could not afford to lose wages on a long voyage.

Another reason for emigration was the active promotion of Canada by agents whose job was to encourage emigration to Canada. By the 1920s Canada had two full time agents based in Glasgow and Inverness.

The Salvation Army also played a part in migration from Scotland. It provided help buying a ticket as well as advice for single women, unemployed men and young people who wanted to emigrate.

Between 1872 and 1930 Quarrier's Orphan Homes of Scotland helped to arrange the migration of 7000 children to Ontario, Canada. For many orphan children emigration was the fresh start they needed in life.

The Empire Settlement Act of 1922 was intended to boost the rural populations of Canada and other parts of the British Empire. Help was given to emigrants who agreed to work the land for a certain amount of time. Both town and country workers seized the opportunity to escape from the grip of depression and unemployment in Scotland.

The 1920s saw more Scots migrating than at any other time in Scotland's history. Emigrants all saw migration as an escape from a Scotland locked in unemployment and decline.

Time to reflect !

A few years ago the singing twins The Proclaimers had a hit song called 'Letter from America'. Try to watch and listen to it on YouTube. Think about how the words and images link to your history course but also what is happening in Scotland today. Does it make a fair comment?

The experience of Scots abroad, 1830s–1939

The fourth part of the syllabus is about the experience of Scots abroad between the 1830s and 1939.

What you should know

To be successful in this section you must be able to:

★ describe ways in which Scots helped develop the new countries they went to
★ describe ways that Scottish identity and culture have been kept alive around the world
★ describe the work of some famous Scots who migrated
★ explain why the emigration of Scots abroad was not always a good thing for local people
★ describe ways in which the British Empire affected Scotland.

Key words

Aborigines – the people who lived in Australia before the arrival of Europeans.
Australasia – the area of Australia, New Zealand, New Guinea and surrounding Pacific islands.
Maoris – the people who lived in New Zealand before the arrival of Europeans.

How did Scots affect the countries that they went to?

Scots who emigrated usually went to countries that were part of the British Empire, such as Canada, Australia, India and New Zealand. Some even went to England!

Scots played an important part in developing the new lands where they settled. Scottish soldiers, farmers, engineers and businessmen were all very important. For example, in Australia Scots made sheep grazing and the wool trade big business. In India, Lord Dalhousie introduced many changes to the lives of Indians. In the 1920s, many Scots took their engineering skills south to England and worked in the new car making industry.

Scots emigrants took with them their customs and culture. Pipe bands, highland dress, highland games and Burns clubs appeared wherever Scots settled. Scottish place names are still common in Australasia and Canada.

Famous Scottish emigrants

Scots such as John Muir and Andrew Carnegie are examples of successful Scots emigrants.

Andrew Carnegie, born in Dunfermline, Fife, made a fortune through hard work in the USA then spent most of it trying to help others, both in the USA and in Scotland.

John Muir, born in Dunbar, East Lothian, was an environmentalist and conservationist long before these ideas became fashionable. He helped create Yellowstone National Park in the USA.

Andrew Fisher was born in East Ayrshire, Scotland and migrated to Queensland in 1885. Within 25 years Fisher became Australian Prime Minister and worked on creating the law-making system of the new country called Australia.

The effect of immigration on native peoples

Scots were also involved in things that would be disapproved of today. Many took land by force from the native peoples of North America and Australasia. These Scots were in turn doing to others what had been done to them. Native Americans, Aborigines and Maoris were cleared off their land to make way for immigrants. Ironically, in Australia the immigrants cleared local aboriginal people out of their homeland to make way for sheep farms.

Time to reflect !

Do people migrating to another country have a right to change or influence the country they go to? If you say yes do you try to control what changes they can make? Do you think immigrants coming to Scotland now and in the future should expect to change it?

Do your answers to these questions help you understand the reaction of native peoples to Scottish immigrants in the past?

For practice

The following questions are examples of the types of questions you can expect within each of the three parts of the syllabus.

Immigration to Scotland between the 1830s and 1939

How fully does Source A explain why Irish people were attracted to emigrate to Scotland in the nineteenth century? (6 marks)

Source A is from an official report written in 1836:

> A large number of Irish have arrived in Great Britain in recent years. The wages they are able to earn here are almost always higher than they could earn in their own country. Moreover the employment is more regular. This means that in Scotland they are able to obtain payment on a greater number of days in the year. There is also more chance of getting employment for women and children in the manufacturing towns.

It is a good idea to start by writing that the source partly explains a situation. This allows you to go on to show what *is* and what *is not* in the source ⇨

⇨

The source mentions that, in Scotland:

- people could usually earn higher wages
- there was more regular employment
- work was also available for women and children.

However the source does not mention that:

- there were short, regular crossings from Ireland to Scotland
- the fares were cheaper to Scotland than to other places
- many emigrants already had relatives living in Scotland
- the growth of industry in central Scotland provided many new jobs.

The immigrant experience in Scotland, 1830s–1939

To what extent was religious difference the main reason why Scots disliked Irish immigrants? (9 marks)

Write a short introduction showing you understand there were other factors apart from the religious difference which contributed to the Scots' dislike of Irish immigrants. List these factors in your introduction.

You should then explain why religious difference was important. For example:

- most Scots were Protestant and most Irish were Catholic so religious rivalry was likely
- some Scots resented the way the Catholic church seemed to encourage immigrants not to integrate
- newspapers and books stirred up anti-Catholic feeling.

You should then balance your answer by giving other reasons why Scots disliked Irish immigrants.

- Irish immigrants were blamed for shortages of housing
- they were blamed for keeping down wages
- they were accused of drunkenness and crime.

You should finish with a conclusion that gives an overall answer to the question and support it with a reason for the judgement you have made. For example:

The religious difference was the main reason why Scots disliked Irish immigrants. Protestant Irish immigrants did not suffer the hatred that was stirred up against Catholic Irish immigrants.

Evaluate the usefulness of Source B as evidence about the experience of Irish immigrants in Scotland. (5 marks)

Source B is by a Roman Catholic Bishop of Scotland giving evidence in 1836 to the Inquiry into the Irish Poor in Britain:

> A few have succeeded in raising themselves to the rank of respectable shopkeeper, there are several who keep whisky shops. The bulk of the male population are weavers or labourers on the roads, canals, coal pits, draining, ditching, coal porters etc and the female population is usually employed at the steam looms or in the cotton mills.

You need to make **five** clear points about the usefulness of the source.

You would probably start by arguing that the source does provide useful evidence about the experience of Irish immigrants.

You should comment on who wrote the source, when it was written and why it was written. You must also state why each of the points you are writing about makes the source useful as evidence. You could mention that:

- the source was written by a Catholic bishop, who is likely to take an interest in the welfare of Irish immigrants
- it was written by a bishop giving evidence to an inquiry so it is likely to be a truthful account
- the source was written in 1836 at a time when many Irish people had come to settle in Scotland.

You should then comment on the information contained in the source:

- The source tells us that some Irish own their own businesses (i.e. shopkeepers)
- It tells us that most males laboured (worked) in textiles, transport and mining
- It says that women worked in the textile industry.

You could decide, however, that in some ways the source is less useful because of important information that has not been mentioned, for example, that:

- most Irish did low paid work in poor conditions
- many experienced poor living conditions
- Irish immigrants faced hostility from the Scottish population.

Scottish emigration, 1830s–1939

Explain the reasons why many Highland Scots chose to go overseas in the nineteenth century. (6 marks)

You need to make **six** separate points from recall. You could mention:

- the continuing difficulties of farming in the Highlands, e.g. climate, soil
- the growing population in the early nineteenth century
- the impact of the potato blight
- that landowners evicted tenants to make way for sheep and then deer
- the failure of industries, e.g. kelp
- that some Highlanders already had relatives abroad
- landowner/government support for emigration.

You can always gain an extra mark if you bring in more information to back up a point you are making. For example: *Highland Scots chose to go overseas because of continuing difficulties of farming in the Highlands* (1 mark). *There was a lack of cultivatable soil in many of the Highland glens* (1 extra mark).

The experience of Scots abroad, 1830s–1939

To what extent was the success of Scottish emigrants abroad due to their business skills? (9 marks)

Write a short introduction showing you understand there were other factors which contributed to the success of Scottish emigrants abroad. List these factors in your introduction.

You should then explain why business skills were important. For example:

- Scots had experience working in banking
- Scots showed the ability to invest money wisely
- Scots brought knowledge of textile manufacturing, mining and steel making.

You should then balance your answer by giving other reasons for the success of Scots:

- Scots showed political skills
- Scots were often better educated
- Scots had a reputation for hard work.

You should finish with a conclusion giving an overall answer to the question and support it with a reason for the judgement you have made.

For example: *Overall, their education was more important in explaining the success of Scottish emigrants as this was something almost all Scottish emigrants had but which other emigrants did not share.*

Compare the views in Sources C and D on the reasons for the success of Scottish emigrants abroad. (4 marks)

In **Sources C** and **D** modern historians explain the success of Scots abroad.

Source C

> Scots who settled abroad had a range of skills that few other emigrants could match. An added bonus was that they often arrived in their new countries with some money to invest. The famous traditions of Scottish education were also important to their success. Some Scots arrived with the traditional craftsmen's skills which are now seen as a key factor in the Scottish dominance of much of Canadian industry.

Source D

> Scots who settled in Canada carved themselves a place in history as inventors and engineers. James McGill, a Glasgow fur trader, invested much of his wealth in the University in Montreal which still bears his name. Alexander Graham Bell, who was born in Scotland and was educated in Edinburgh, emigrated to Canada and is remembered around the world as the inventor who perfected the telephone.

For this type of question you must say whether you think the sources agree or not and then support your decision either by making 4 simple comparisons stating what the sources agree or disagree on, or by supporting your comparison with evidence from the sources – this is called a developed comparison. Two developed comparisons are worth the full 4 marks.

For this question you would probably decide that the two sources agree. You could then back this up with two of the following comparisons:

- Source C says that Scots had a range of skills and Source D supports this by saying that they became famous inventors and engineers.
- Source C points out that Scots often brought money to invest and Source D backs this up by mentioning James McGill, who invested money in the University of Montreal.
- Source C says that Scottish education was important to their success and Source D supports this by pointing out that Alexander Graham Bell was educated in Edinburgh.

Scots on the Western Front

The first part of the syllabus is about Scots on the Western Front.

What you should know

To be successful in this section you must be able to:
- ★ explain why many young Scots joined the army in 1914
- ★ describe life in the trenches on the Western Front
- ★ describe the effect of technology on soldiers and military tactics on the Western Front.

Key words

Artillery – very large guns that could fire heavy explosive shells long distances.

Attrition – wearing down the enemy so that they cannot stay in the war any longer.

Recruitment – persuading young men to join the army.

Western Front – the area of fighting in Belgium and Northern France.

Recruitment

The British army was very small compared to other countries' armies. As soon as the war started, a recruiting campaign also started. Its purpose was to persuade young men to join the army.

Recruitment posters could be seen everywhere. All across Scotland, young men were urged to join the army through a mixture of peer pressure, feelings of guilt, honour and patriotism. Many posters in Scotland played on the attractions of tartan, kilts and the warlike history of Scottish clans. Kitchener's campaign was a huge success. More Scots volunteered in proportion to the size of the population than from any other area of the UK.

Experience of life in the trenches

Trenches were dug stretching 400 miles from the English Channel to the Swiss frontier. Soldiers knew they were at risk every moment from a mortar shell or sniper fire. Apart from the fear and danger of attacks, soldiers also had to cope with noise, itching, boredom and mud.

Scottish troops gained a reputation as hard fighters and were often used as 'shock troops', to hit the enemy hard in the opening moments of a battle. Bagpipe music was often used to inspire the troops at the start of an attack. Piper Laidlaw provided such music at the historic Battle of Loos.

The kilted regiments suffered a great deal from lice in the pleats of their kilts and many hours were spent trying to 'pop' the eggs of lice by candlelight.

As the war went on Scottish 'kilties' were given khaki aprons to wrap around over their kilts to provide camouflage.

The Germans called the kilted regiments 'the ladies from hell'.

However, soldiers did not live in the trenches all the time. A soldier in a front line trench on a Monday would usually be 'rotated' back to a rest and recovery position by the following weekend. Of course, by the next weekend they would be going back to the front line again.

Military tactics

Both sides created trench networks defended by machine guns and barbed wire. The result was that neither side could break through, leading to a stalemate.

The battles on the Western Front, such as the Somme and Verdun, were battles of attrition. The attacking side knew that they would suffer huge casualties, but the hope was that the opposition would be worn down and, eventually, that is what happened to Germany. By November 1918 Germany did not have the food, resources or men to continue with the war.

The technology of war

Machine guns were not new weapons but they became more deadly as the war went on. Artillery also destroyed soldiers. It is thought that up to 75 per cent of **all** deaths and casualties in the war were caused by artillery.

The first example of a new technology that was used to try and break the deadlock was gas. At first, poison gas panicked defenceless soldiers but was not a 'breakthrough' weapon. Early gas attacks relied heavily on the wind to blow the gas into the enemy positions. But what if the wind changed? Eventually gas shells were fired by artillery. The main reason gas ceased to be effective was that gas masks were quickly developed.

Tanks were developed in Britain and the idea was good – a strong metal vehicle that could cross no-man's land, burst through barbed wire and was immune to machine gun bullets. Tanks could also provide cover for advancing soldiers. In reality, the tanks were slow, they often broke down and conditions inside the tanks were horrible. By 1918, however, tanks had improved. At Amiens and Cambrai in 1918 tanks were used in a co-ordinated way on firm ground and were a huge advantage.

By the closing months of the war three developments had emerged:
1 Radio communication had improved. It was now possible to organise an integrated attack.
2 The quality of tanks had improved greatly.
3 Aircraft could be used to support attacking troops. Early in the war, planes were used to scout enemy positions and sometimes got into 'dog fights' with enemy aircraft. Later in the war integrated attacks using a combination of tanks, aircraft, artillery and infantry were developed. This happened at the battle of Amiens in August 1918 just before the German surrender.

Time to reflect !

The war made both sides think of ways of breaking the deadlock and also how their weapons could be made more effective. Was victory the result of developing new technology and changing tactics, or was the defeat of Germany really the result of long battles of attrition?

The Great War and everyday life in Scotland

The second part of the syllabus is about how the First World War affected everyday life in Scotland.

What you should know

To be successful in this section you must be able to:

★ describe the changing role of women during the war
★ explain why conscription was introduced and what conscientious objectors were
★ describe the effect of high casualties and deaths on Scottish society
★ explain why propaganda and rationing were necessary during wartime.

Propaganda

During the war the government tried to control how people felt about the war. They used propaganda to involve people in the war, either to support their own side or to encourage hatred of the other side. By repeating certain messages such as 'don't waste food' and 'lend the government your savings' the government tried to persuade the people to do what they wanted.

Rationing

Rationing was started so that everyone could be sure of a regular and sufficient food supply. An organised system of rationing could also control the price of basic foods.

By the end of 1917, it was clear that Britain was facing serious food shortages due to the targeting by German submarines of all merchant ships carrying food to Britain. In January 1918, the government began a system of rationing and by April 1918 full scale rationing was in force in Scotland. By the end of the war almost all food prices were controlled by the government.

Conscription

The government passed the Military Service Act in January 1916. The new law enforced conscription for single men between the ages of 19 and 40. In May 1916 conscription was extended to married men and by 1918 men up to the age of 50 were being conscripted.

In Britain, supporters of conscription argued that young men had a duty, above all else, to defend their country. On the other hand, those against conscription argued that it had not been used in Britain before and that its introduction meant another increase in the power of the government at the cost of individual liberty.

Key words

Absolutists – conscientious objectors who refused absolutely to do anything to help the war effort.

Commemorate – to remember people who were killed in the war by creating memorials and holding ceremonies.

Conscientious objectors – men who refused to obey the conscription law.

Conscription – making young men join the army by law.

Exemption – to be excused from something or be let off from doing something.

Memorial – a symbol of the losses suffered by people during the war so that their names are not forgotten.

Munitions – all the ammunition, shells and explosive devices used during the war.

Pacifists – people who oppose any form of fighting in a war for whatever reason.

Propaganda – exaggerated stories or lies meant to make people hate the enemy or support their own side without question.

Rationing – controlling the supply of food so that everyone gets a fair share.

The London Scottish Regiment undergoing rifle drill.

Some men refused to accept conscription. They were called 'conscientious objectors' and claimed exemption on grounds of their political or religious beliefs.

They were usually sent to military units and if they refused to obey the order of an officer, they were court-martialled, where they risked being sentenced to death. However, that did not happen. Around 7000 conscientious objectors agreed to perform non-combat duties, often as stretcher-bearers on the front line. However, more than 1500 pacifists were 'absolutists' who opposed doing any work that helped Britain's war effort. These were sent to prison in the UK where they were kept in very harsh conditions. During the war, 69 conscientious objectors died in prison.

Both during and after the war ended very few people had sympathy for conscientious objectors.

Women's war work

With so many men away fighting, women were encouraged to replace the missing men. Industries that had previously excluded women now welcomed them. Women worked as conductors on trams and buses, as typists and secretaries in offices and in factories and nearly 200,000 women found work in government departments. The biggest increase in female employment was in the previously male dominated engineering industry, especially the part that made munitions. Before the war, fewer than 4000 women worked in heavy industry in Scotland. By 1917 over 30,000 women were employed making munitions in Scotland.

When the war ended the majority of women did not keep their wartime jobs. A new law called the Restoration of Pre-War Practices Act meant that returning soldiers were given back their jobs. Women were forced to leave the 'men's work' jobs which they had done during the war years. The idea that a woman's place was in the home was as strong as it had ever been.

Casualties and memorials

After four years of war, the Scottish population wanted some way to commemorate their dead. In the years that followed the Great War, towns and villages across Scotland built their own memorials to remember and commemorate their own losses. There was also a demand for a national memorial. Scotland's National War Memorial stands in Crown Square within Edinburgh Castle and the opening ceremony took place on 14 July 1927. The people of Scotland hoped that the dead had not died in vain and that the Great War really would be the war to end all wars.

The effect of the Great War on Scottish industry and the economy

The third part of the syllabus is about how the First World War affected Scottish industry and the economy.

Time to reflect !

Before the war many people may never have thought about the relationship between themselves and their government. In what ways did the war cause people to think about their duties to their country and also their rights and freedoms as citizens of the country? Do such thoughts matter?

What you should know

To be successful in this section you must be able to:

★ describe the main features of Scotland's industry and economy before the First World War
★ explain how the war gave a wartime boost to Scottish industry and the economy
★ describe the post-war decline of heavy industry.

Key words

'New' industries – industries that started just before or after the war. They included car-making, electronics, chemicals and making radios.

Post-war – the years right after the end of the war.

Industry

In 1914, Scotland led the world in shipbuilding and engineering, and in the production of coal, iron and steel but there were signs that all was not well. Scotland relied too heavily on these handful of 'heavy industries', which employed most of Scotland's workforce. Each of the heavy industries relied on the others' success.

At first the war provided a temporary boost for Scotland's industries. Heavy industry was vital to make the weapons of war. However, the demand for production during the war years made the fall in demand much worse when it came during the post-war years.

By the end of the First World War it was clear that new industries were becoming very important, especially in electronics, radio, car and aircraft production as well as the chemical industry. The problem for Scotland was that these 'new' industries developed in the south of England and did little to help employment in Scotland.

War work and reserved occupations

The government was worried that because so many men had rushed to join the army many important jobs that were needed for the war effort, such as coal mining, might not have enough workers.

When conscription was introduced the government was keen to ensure that 'essential workers' remained at work. The answer was 'reserved occupations'. A reserved occupation meant people doing certain jobs could not be called up for the army.

The government was deliberately vague about what jobs would be classed as reserved. They feared that many men would rush to these jobs in a bid to avoid the call up.

Time to reflect !

Do you think the war helped the Scottish economy, made it worse or just postponed the inevitable?

The Great War and politics in Scotland

The fourth part of the syllabus is about how the First World War affected politics in Scotland.

What you should know

To be successful in this section you must be able to:

★ describe how the war affected the campaigns for votes for women
★ explain what is meant by 'Red Clydeside'
★ describe the Defence of the Realm Act and the reaction in Scotland to it
★ explain why the war led to more people being given the right to vote
★ describe what was meant by 'homes fit for heroes'.

The campaigns for women's suffrage

Before 1918 women had no national political voice. They had no vote. Organised campaigns for women's suffrage began in 1866 but some men (and women) thought women were often irrational, emotional and not suited to politics! By 1900 women, especially middle-class women, were better educated, often at universities, and were allowed to vote in local elections. Countries such as New Zealand had given the vote to women, so why not Britain?

In 1897, a number of local women's suffrage societies formed the National Union of Women's Suffrage Societies (NUWSS). The NUWSS believed in peaceful tactics to win the vote, mainly for middle-class, property-owning women. The NUWSS was nicknamed the Suffragists. Membership of the NUWSS remained high and when the Suffragettes (see below) became more violent, membership of the NUWSS rocketed as women left the Women's Social and Political Union (WSPU)!

In 1903 the WSPU was formed, led by Emmeline Pankhurst. The WSPU was nicknamed the Suffragettes. Their motto was 'deeds not words' and at first they grabbed the headlines through largely peaceful demonstrations. However, from 1910 onwards, the Suffragettes became

Key words

Rent – money paid to the owners of property (called landlords) by the people who lived in the properties (called tenants).

Rent strike – a refusal by women in Glasgow, then across central Scotland, to pay increases in rents for their homes.

Slums – areas of very bad quality housing that usually also led to bad health for the people who lived in them.

Subsidy – money paid by the government towards the total cost of building new houses.

Suffrage – the right to vote.

more militant, which means they used more violent methods of protest, such as firebombs and attacks on politicians. They also went on hunger strikes and the resulting Cat and Mouse Act made big headlines in newspapers.

The actions of the Suffragettes destroyed sympathy for the issue of votes for women among some MPs who had previously supported it. The Suffragettes also ignored the thousands of working-class men who still had no political voice. Mrs Pankhurst was even willing to settle for granting the vote to some wealthy women rather than campaign for the vote for all adults.

When war broke out in 1914, the WSPU suspended campaigning. Instead of 'Votes for Women', Pankhurst formed the Britannia Society and adopted the slogan 'The Right to Serve'. The Suffragists also stopped campaigning explicitly, although ambulances sponsored by the NUWSS appeared on the front line just to maintain awareness of the role of women.

The war opened up jobs to women that would otherwise have been closed to them. Furthermore, in 1918 the Representation of the People Act gave the vote to eight million women over the age of 30 (and to an additional thirteen million men). However, the women who had worked long hours and risked their lives in munitions factories were mostly single, in their late teens or early 20s and they were not given the vote in 1918. They had to wait until 1928 when the vote was given to all men and women who were 21 and over.

'Red Clydeside'

The words Red Clydeside refers to the years between 1915 and 1919 when protests and demonstrations by workers in the Glasgow area made it look as if a revolution might break out.

- RED was a word used to describe communist revolutionaries. They flew the red flag of revolution.
- CLYDESIDE is the area around Glasgow and the river Clyde where the protests and demonstrations took place.

By 1915 tension and suspicion between workers on one side and government on the other was high. From the workers' point of view, the actions of the government seemed aimed at cutting wages, making the working hours longer and bringing in unskilled women workers to do the jobs of highly skilled engineers. From the government's point of view, the workers on the Clyde were a nest of revolutionaries ready to upset the war effort and even lead revolution in Britain.

Things calmed down until the war ended when returning soldiers faced unemployment. On the Clyde, trades unions tried to change working hours so that soldiers who came back looking for **their old jobs could find work.**

In January 1919 a big protest was planned for George Square, Glasgow. On Friday 30 January at least 90,000 workers had gathered in George Square when the police launched a baton charge on the crowd. A running battle started between the police and demonstrators. Over 12,000 English troops were brought in by the government to restore order.

Within a week of the 'battle of George Square', the strike was over. Some people claim that this event was the closest Britain came to revolution, but the strike leaders only ever claimed they wanted a reduction of the working week and more jobs available for returning soldiers. Red Clydeside was a good name to generate publicity, but in reality there was never any threat of a revolution starting in Glasgow.

DORA

DORA was a law that allowed the government to do many things to protect the country during the war. It was really called the Defence of the Realm Act.

At first the public accepted the need for increased security and control over things that were seen to be vital for the war effort. However, as the war went on, the public became tired of restrictions that seemed only to have a slight connection with the war effort. For example, DORA limited the opening times of pubs and reduced the alcoholic strength of beer.

More seriously, people objected to the way that DORA gave the government the right to imprison people without trial, something which was directly against the freedoms that British people had struggled to win over many years.

Women and the rent strikes

The Great War is often seen as a major turning point in the role of women in British society. It also made many women more willing to fight for their rights.

The rent strikes of 1915 became an example of how people could take action to fight against unfairness. More importantly, the rent strikes became an example of how women could campaign for change and succeed!

Demand for housing in and around Glasgow rocketed because of in-coming war workers. Landlords threatened to raise the rents on their properties to cash in on the rising demand. The landlords hoped that with most men away in the army, the women would just give in. But, faced with rising food prices and rising rents, some women decided to fight back.

In May 1915 the first rent strike began and men in the engineering factories went on strike to support the women. Soon, the government was under pressure to act. Their response was the Rent Restriction Act. Rents were frozen at 1914 levels unless improvements had been made to the property.

The women's demands had been met and the strikers had learned an important lesson: direct action could lead to positive results.

'Homes fit for heroes'

Towards the end of the war the Prime Minister, David Lloyd George, needed support from the British voters. He believed that once the war was won people would vote for the political party that offered better living conditions.

Before the First World War the majority of the houses available to rent by the lower-paid were often just slums. As the war reached its end politicians promised that soldiers would not return to the bad housing they had left. The returning soldiers were promised 'homes fit for heroes to live in'.

The Housing Act of 1919 was the first time that the government provided some money to local councils to help build council houses for working-class people. However, the subsidy given by the government was not enough for the local councils to buy the land to build on and provide the building materials.

The result was that the 'cheap' rent charged for the houses was still too expensive for poor families, who could not afford to pay the rents.

The Housing Act of 1919 promised to build 500,000 houses within three years but in reality only half that number were built.

> **Time to reflect** !
>
> At the end of the war people spoke about returning to the 'good old days' of before the war. How would you have felt in 1919?

For practice

The following questions are examples of the types of questions you can expect within each of the three parts of the syllabus.

Scots on the Western Front

How fully does Source A explain why so many Scots volunteered for the armed forces in 1914? (6 marks)

Source A is about the recruitment campaign to the armed forces in 1914.

> At first the outbreak of war was exciting for many Scots. The opportunity to go on an adventure with your pals in a kilted uniform was too good to miss. There were more Scots volunteers in proportion to the size of the population than any other area of the UK. War hysteria also played a part. The War Propaganda Bureau told stories of Belgian babies being bayoneted and nurses and nuns being raped by German soldiers.

It is a good idea to introduce your answer by saying that the source explains the situation fairly well. This allows you to go on to show what **is** and what **is not** in the source.

You can support this introduction by saying the source mentions that:

- at first the war was exciting
- peer pressure encouraged men to join up
- people were influenced by anti-German propaganda.

However, the source does not mention important points such as:

- the strong military tradition in parts of Scotland
- that people responded to the strong appeal to patriotism
- that many Scots faced poverty and unemployment which encouraged them to enlist.

Explain the reasons for the high casualties caused by artillery on the Western Front. (6 marks)

You need to give **six** reasons to explain why artillery caused high casualties:

You could mention:

- the devastating effects of shrapnel
- that artillery pieces fired from distance, which gave them the advantage of surprise and made retaliation difficult
- the use of aircraft to range the guns
- that trenches offered little protection against a direct hit
- the intensity of artillery bombardments/large numbers used in major bombardments
- that artillery noise caused shell-shock.

You can always gain an extra mark if you bring in more information to back up a point you are making. For example: *High casualties were caused by the devastating effects of shrapnel* (1 mark). *These metal fragments could cause casualties hundreds of metres away from the shell explosion* (1 extra mark).

The Great War and everyday life in Scotland

Evaluate the usefulness of Source B as evidence of the effects of the war on women. (5 marks)

Source B is a poster produced by the Ministry for Food in 1917. You need to make **five** clear points about the usefulness of the source.

You would probably start by arguing that the source does provide useful evidence about the effects of the war on women. You should comment on who wrote the source, when it was written and why it was written. You must also state why each of the points you are writing about makes the source useful as evidence.

You could mention that:

- the source was produced by the Ministry of Food, which gave advice to women about food during the war
- it was produced in 1917 when food became very scarce
- it was produced to encourage women to save food.

You should then comment on the information contained in the source:

- it shows that women were under pressure to save food
- it shows that women were part of the war effort and that they could help to defeat the U-boat campaign
- it shows that women were given advice on how to save food.

However, you could decide that in some ways the source is less useful because of important information that has not been mentioned, for example:

- it doesn't show that women were affected in many other ways, e.g. war work
- it doesn't show that women's lives improved in some ways, e.g. higher pay.

The effect of the Great War on Scottish industry and the economy

To what extent was the war to blame for the decline of heavy industry during the 1920s? (9 marks)

Write a short introduction showing you understand there were other factors which contributed to the decline of heavy industry. List these factors in your introduction.

You should then explain why the war was important. You could mention that:

- many Scottish businesses lost their overseas markets
- foreign competition increased during the war, e.g. growth of textile industry in India during war
- businesses were concentrating on war production
- the war caused a decline in international trade.

You should then balance your answer by giving other reasons for the decline. For example:

- new industries failed to take root in Scotland after war
- there was a lack of investment in new technology in Scotland's heavy industry
- employers failed to train their workforce in new skills.

You should finish with a conclusion that gives an overall answer to the question and support it with a reason for the judgement you have made.

For example: *Overall, the war was mainly to blame for the decline of heavy industry because so many customers for British goods had to buy them elsewhere while the war was on.*

The Great War and politics in Scotland

Describe the impact of DORA on the Scottish people. (4 marks)

You need to make **four** separate points from recall. You could mention that:

- there was an increase in press censorship
- the government took greater control over industry, e.g. munitions
- restrictions were placed on the sale of alcohol
- the demand for increased food production had a major impact on farmers/crofters
- people suspected of damaging the war effort could be imprisoned without trial
- restrictions were placed on the right to strike
- wartime restrictions had a major impact on life in Scottish coastal towns.

You can always gain an extra mark if you bring in more information to back up a point you are making.

For example: *DORA led to an increase in press censorship* (1 mark). *Newspapers were prevented from carrying details of the fighting at the front in case it affected morale at home* (1 extra mark).

Compare the views in Sources C and D about what happened on Clydeside in 1919. (4 marks)

Sources C and **D** describe what happened on Clydeside in 1919.

Source C

> The government was right to expect a socialist rising and it should have taken place. The workers were ready and able to carry it out. The mistake we made on Friday 31st January was marching to the centre of Glasgow. If we had gone to the barracks at Maryhill we could easily have persuaded the soldiers to support us and Clydeside would have been in our hands.

Source D

> The government was worried about the loyalty of the police and armed forces in Glasgow. Had the government understood the situation better they could have saved themselves and the country a lot of bother. The leaders of the movement had no real support for their plans. The day after their protests in George Square the strikers went to the football just as they always did. They were not interested in a socialist take over.

For this type of question you must say whether you think the sources agree or not and then support your decision either by making 4 simple comparisons stating what the sources agree or disagree on, or by supporting your comparison with evidence from the sources – this is called a developed comparison. Two developed comparisons are worth the full 4 marks.

For this question you would probably decide that the two sources disagree. You could then back this up with two of the following comparisons:

- Source C says that the government was right to expect a rising but Source D says the government misunderstood the situation.
- Source C says that the workers were ready and able to carry out a rising but Source D claims there was no real support among the workers.
- Source C says that if tactics had been different Clydeside would have been taken over by the workers but Source D says there was no interest in a socialist take over.

Chapter 5

The Atlantic slave trade and the triangular trade

The first part of the syllabus is about the Atlantic slave trade and the triangular trade.

What you should know

To be successful in this section you must be able to:

★ describe what the Atlantic slave trade was
★ explain how the triangular trade operated
★ describe conditions on the middle passage.

The Atlantic slave trade

The Atlantic slave trade lasted from the sixteenth century through to the nineteenth century. It meant taking Africans as slaves across the Atlantic Ocean from the west coast of Africa to the USA or the Caribbean.

The triangular trade

The Transatlantic slave trade was called the triangular trade as it roughly resembled the shape of a triangle. Ships travelled in three stages:

Stage 1

The first stage of the trade involved ships travelling from Europe carrying manufactured goods such as guns, cloth and alcohol to West Africa. There the slave traders would trade their cargoes for slaves. When the ships were full, the slave ships would travel to the Americas.

Stage 2

The second stage was known as the middle passage and it involved the transportation of captured Africans across the Atlantic to be sold as slaves. During the voyages across the Atlantic the ships' holds were packed with captives. Historians think that approximately 10 million Africans were enslaved by Europeans over the whole period of the slave trade and approximately 10 million more died during the process of capture and transportation in the middle passage.

Stage 3

The third stage of the triangular trade was the return journey to Europe from the Americas. Once the slaves were sold, the money raised was used to buy things that were in big demand in Europe such as tobacco, cotton

Key words

The Americas – in this book it means an area that includes the Caribbean islands and the southern states of the USA.
The middle passage – the part of the triangular trade that carried captive Africans to the Americas to be sold as slaves.
Transatlantic – across the Atlantic Ocean.

Hints & tips

In this section you should ensure you are able to describe the terrible treatment and conditions of slaves on the middle passage. The case of the Zong would be a good example to use.

You should also be able to explain the difference between 'close pack' and 'tight pack' in terms of loading slaves on board. Look at the the diagram on page 40 of the Brookes ship to give you an idea of basic conditions.

and sugar. For nearly 100 years sugar remained Britain's largest and most valuable import from the Americas.

What was the effect of the slave trade on Africa?

What was Africa Like?

Slavery was not new to Africa. It was not started by European traders.

The civilisations of Ancient Egypt, Greece and Rome all enslaved people from Africa. During the Middle Ages, Arabs built an empire across northern Africa and into Europe. They enslaved people to work for them, mainly as servants in their homes.

During the Middle Ages, Arab traders crossed the Sahara Desert to trade in western Africa. They brought back gold, ivory and enslaved people.

The Atlantic slave trade

Portuguese explorers first sailed down the west coast of Africa around 1540. They were looking for gold and ivory. They found Africans buying and selling slaves and started to join in with this trade.

The development of sugar plantations in the West Indies during the seventeenth and eighteenth centuries created a demand for slaves. European traders took more and more enslaved people from West Africa.

In some places the African rulers tried to prevent the trade of slaves but in other places the rulers encouraged it. Some rulers captured African people from other tribes and sold them to European traders.

Experts have estimated that if there had been no slave trade the population of Africa in 1850 would have been 50 million instead of 25 million. The loss of so many people is likely to have worsened the effects of natural disasters such as famine and disease because having fewer healthy young people to produce food would make famine more likely and the death toll worse.

The movement of enslaved people and the trade of goods across Africa led to improvements in transport networks to the coast. Atlantic slavery also led to some improvements in farming but this was to provide food for the slave ships and not to feed the local population.

The slave trade encouraged conflict between tribes. Most of the enslaved Africans who were sold to Europeans were prisoners of war. The demand for greater numbers of enslaved people led to increased hatred and violence between communities in Africa.

What was the effect of the slave trade on British ports?

Many British ports benefited from the wealth of the triangular trade. However, 90 per cent of the ships involved in the trade left from one of three ports: London, Bristol or Liverpool.

London

From 1663 until 1698 London was the only British port that was allowed to trade in African slaves. After 1698, merchants from other British ports became more involved in Atlantic slavery and by 1730, ships from Bristol were carrying more enslaved people than London vessels.

While London became less important as a port for slave ships, London merchants found other ways of making fortunes from the triangular trade. From the late 1600s to the early1800s, the demand for financial services such as insurance and long-term loans created new opportunities for making money.

Merchants involved in the triangular trade also needed insurance. The City of London provided the financial services which were vital for the success of Atlantic slavery.

Bristol

Bristol's west coast position gave it an advantage over London in the trade with Ireland, France, Spain and Portugal.

The city boomed because of its slave-trading success. Merchants spent money on fine new buildings in the centre of the city. Industries such as copper-smelting, sugar-refining and glass-making grew as a result of the slave trade.

Liverpool

Before it became involved in the slave trade, Liverpool was a poor city with a port that was not very successful. By the 1780s, Liverpool had become the largest slave-ship construction site in Britain and the city had been transformed into a prosperous trading centre.

Liverpool, unlike Bristol, had a very large deep waterfront, easily accessible to the ships of the day and not affected by the tides. Ships could be unloaded and reloaded much more quickly than in Bristol and larger ships had no difficulties docking at Liverpool, so their owners preferred to use that port.

Was Scotland involved in the slave trade?

Scotland was independent until 1707 and was not allowed to take part in the growing trade with English colonies in the West Indies. However, Scotland played an important role in West Indian slavery which has, to some extent, been hidden.

It was common for Scottish vessels to travel to West Africa via European ports such as Rotterdam to load trade goods. Glasgow merchants made a lot of money dealing in American tobacco, which was mainly produced by African slaves but the Glasgow merchants traded only the tobacco, not the slaves themselves. Only around 30 slave voyages departed from Scottish ports and most of these left from Greenock and Port Glasgow.

Time to reflect

Today there is a feeling that the triangular trade should be acknowledged by triangular guilt. That means that each part of the trade – the Europeans, the West Africans and the West Indians – should all apologise for the part played by their ancestors in the slave trade. Do you agree with that point of view?

The importance of the slave trade to Britain and the Caribbean

The second part of the syllabus is about the importance of the slave trade to Britain and the Caribbean.

What you should know

To be successful in this section you must be able to:

★ explain why slavery in the Americas was such a vital part of the British economy
★ describe examples of how Britain benefitted from the slave trade
★ describe the main products produced on the slave plantations
★ explain why those products were so valued in Europe.

The climate and land on the Caribbean islands and in the southern states of the USA made the growing of crops such as sugar, cotton and tobacco possible. These crops were grown on big farms called plantations. Until the nineteenth century, slaves from Africa were used to work on plantations.

The most important crop in Britain's West Indian colonies was sugar. Growing sugar cane is hard, heavy work. Slaves cut the sugar cane and transported it to the mill, where the cane was crushed and boiled to extract its juice. In the eighteenth century, slaves only survived for about four years working on the sugar plantations.

The colony of Virginia was Britain's first permanent settlement in North America. Due to the colony's Scottish connections and the easy route from Scotland to Virginia, Glasgow became an important port for tobacco imports to Britain.

The slave trade and the British economy

Slave ships had to be built, fitted out and repaired. Dock workers, blacksmiths, carpenters, sail-makers and rope-makers worked all year round on Britain's slave trade fleet. Chains and shackles were needed for use on the slaves and banking and insurance companies supplied services to slave merchants.

Greenock, near Glasgow, had one of the largest sugar companies in the world. Glasgow merchants owned the plantations in Virginia, growing the tobacco used in huge factories around Glasgow making cigarettes.

Elsewhere in Britain, Birmingham was the largest gun-producing town partly because it supplied guns to be traded for slaves, while 75 per cent of all sugar produced in the plantations came to London to supply the very fashionable coffee houses.

Meanwhile, thousands of Britons made their living from processing the raw sugar, cotton and tobacco.

While the produce of the Caribbean made Britain rich, back in the Caribbean the plantation owners made a fortune and lived in luxury. Caribbean ports and agencies supporting the slave trade also grew and became prosperous but wealth was always in the hands of a few white businessmen.

The Atlantic slave trade had a long lasting negative effect on the development of the Caribbean islands.

Their economies were geared up to produce one crop: sugar. When demand fell and sugar prices dropped, the Caribbean islands suffered badly.

The islands were also geared for export to just one country: Britain.

Slavery meant that wealth and power was concentrated in the hands of white plantation owners who stood in the way of progress to protect their position. After Abolition they even tried to keep their plantations going by replacing African slaves with indentured labour from India and China.

The slave trade meant that around 80 per cent of the population of the Caribbean islands were of African origin. Racism and discrimination made it hard for them to get on in life.

They remained poor because they were denied property, education and political rights.

Time to reflect

How does the information you have read in this section affect the arguments about the abolition of slavery? Was slavery a good thing or a bad thing for Britain? Can slavery ever be called a good thing?

Life as a slave and slave resistance

The third part of the syllabus is about what life was like as a slave and asks the question – did slaves ever resist and try to fight back?

What you should know

To be successful in this section you must be able to:

★ describe what happened to captured Africans when they arrived in the Americas
★ describe the type of work done by a slave
★ explain why it was so difficult for slaves to fight back against their conditions.

Captured in Africa

Enslaved people were sold to African middlemen who often acquired slaves many miles from the coast where they were usually sold to a European factor or trader.

The factor often worked for a European trading company. The place where a factor worked was often called a 'slave factory'.

Moving the slaves to the coast often involved a long, hard journey on foot. When they arrived at the coast sometimes enslaved people were kept in large forts. There was a chain of 30 forts along the Gold Coast of West Africa (now called Ghana). They were originally built by Europeans to store gold. Some forts, like the one at Cape Coast, could hold 1000 enslaved people in its cellars.

The enslaved people might be imprisoned for several months while they waited to be put on the slave ships. Conditions on the coast were very bad. Diseases like malaria were common at the mouths of the great rivers.

Key words

Auction – a place where slaves were put on display and sold to the highest bidder.

Christianisation – converting people to believe in the Christian religion.

Indentured – indentured servants were bound to serve their masters, in return for their passage and board. In most cases, they were treated no better than slaves.

Jamaica – a large island in the Caribbean.

Resistance – slaves not accepting their conditions or enslavement and fighting back.

The voyage from West Africa to the Americas became known as the middle passage.

Carpenters worked on the slave ships before they left the African coast and rigged up extra shelving below decks. It was vital to load slaves as efficiently as possible. The human cargo had little or no head room and this made it impossible for them to sit up.

Before being taken on board, slaves often had their heads shaved and their few clothes removed.

Slaves were chained together beneath deck, side by side. They were allowed up on deck for air and exercise for one or two hours a day. They were fed twice a day and given a pint of water.

The voyage itself took between six and eight weeks. The slaves had no idea where they were going or what was going to happen to them. Many deaths on slave journeys across the Atlantic were the result of violence, brawls and, above all, rebellions. There was probably at least one rebellion on every eight to ten journeys.

Slave auctions

Once the slaves landed in the Americas, they were often taken to 'seasoning camps' where they were 'broken in'. That meant breaking their spirit and making them accept their new life as a slave. Mainly, the slaves were beaten and tortured and as many as five million Africans died in these camps.

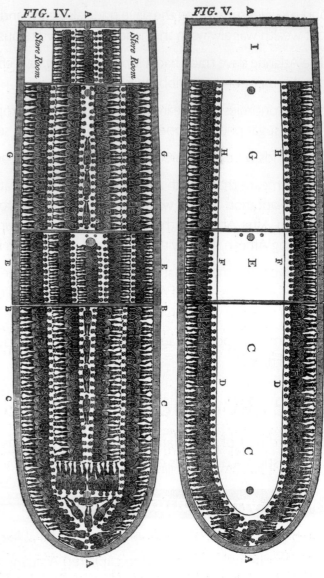

The famous illustration of the Brookes ship showing how slaves were stored on the middle passage.

Slaves were sold to the highest bidder at auction. As far as the slave owner was concerned, the slave was property, not a person.

Slaves were treated harshly and were often kept chained, especially if they were new slaves or likely to run away. Slaves were beaten or whipped often, usually just to frighten the other slaves into obeying their master.

Slave owners tried to keep discipline by appointing an overseer or 'driver'. It was difficult to run away and enslaved people were flogged for the least offence. Enslaved people had to carry a pass or ticket if they left the plantation. The owners kept careful descriptions of all their slaves and usually branded them with red hot irons. The slaves had to grow food for themselves and diseases such as smallpox and dysentery were common.

The majority of slaves were bought to work in the plantation fields. They worked all day, sometimes up to eighteen hours if it was harvest time. They worked in hot sun and lived in basic huts. They were given some food and clothing. Many slaves only survived for four years but they were easily replaced.

Slave resistance

Slaves did resist and even fought back. Resistance started on board the slave ships. Captives on slave ships crossing the Atlantic would take any opportunity to overpower the European crew and take over the ship. One slave ship captain said that at least one in ten ships transporting slaves experienced an uprising.

On the plantation, slaves resisted in different ways:

'In their heads' resistance

Often slaves would keep their real identities alive by continuing customs and habits they had done at home, such as using their real names.

Small-scale resistance

In the colonies, slaves resisted their owners in many ways, such as working slowly or badly, or damaging their owners' property. Some would steal when they got the chance and tried to harm white people. Some enslaved people self-harmed in order to avoid work.

Runaway

Slaves had no idea where they were, nor did they have maps or any knowledge of what was outside their plantation. On small islands there were few places to run to but on larger islands like Jamaica, there were groups of ex-slaves who lived in the mountains.

Punishment

It was important to show slaves being punished as the owners feared a slave revolt. British plantation owners had heard of successful slave revolts in French-owned Haiti, for example, and feared that revolts might spread. By showing what would happen to troublemakers, they hoped the slaves would be too afraid to revolt.

Runaway slaves were hunted and often recaptured. Punishments were severe. Sometimes slaves who kept running away might have toes cut off to stop them from running although they could still work.

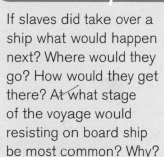

Time to reflect

If slaves did take over a ship what would happen next? Where would they go? How would they get there? At what stage of the voyage would resisting on board ship be most common? Why?

Many slaves were converted to Christianity with its beliefs of love and brotherhood of all people. Some slaves were also taught to read and write. Would those things have had an effect on the attitude of slaves and perhaps encourage resistance?

The abolitionist campaigns to end slavery

The fourth part of the syllabus is about the abolitionist campaigns to end slavery.

What you should know

To be successful you must be able to:
* ★ explain the meanings of 'abolition' and 'abolitionist'
* ★ describe the methods used by abolitionists to gain support for their case
* ★ explain the reasons why many people wanted to keep slavery.

The abolitionist campaigns

In 1787, the Society for the Abolition of the Slave Trade was formed in London. The main leaders of the abolitionist campaign were Thomas Clarkson, Granville Sharp and William Wilberforce. Their main aim was to collect information and evidence that could be presented to parliament to persuade MPs to pass a law that stopped – or abolished – slavery. It was decided to try to end the slave *trade* at first rather than to try to end slavery itself.

The methods of the abolitionists

There had always been people who objected to the slave trade and slavery, but the details of the slave trade were not known by most people. There was no mass media or fast communications at this time so the problem was how to get large numbers of people to support the abolitionist campaign.

The abolitionists knew that success depended on getting massive support from the public. Their methods are still used today in many different protest groups.
- Many people attended meetings organised by abolitionist groups.
- They signed petitions calling for an end to the slave trade.
- They wore anti-slavery badges.
- They refused to buy products from Caribbean or North American colonies where slave labour was used.
- Pamphlets were sold that described the horrors of slavery, especially the middle passage.
- Poetry was also used as a way to spread the message.
- Women and children showed their support by learning and singing abolitionist songs.
- Women wore jewellery that advertised their support for abolition.
- Shoppers chose not to buy goods such as sugar and tobacco produced by slaves.
- An anti-slavery logo was designed showing a kneeling slave with the statement 'Am I not a Man, Am I not a Brother?'
- Petitions were collected and sent to parliament. In Edinburgh in 1792, 3685 men signed a petition. When it was unrolled, the petition stretched the entire length of the House of Commons floor.
- A famous picture was produced called the *Brookes Ship*. It showed how the captured Africans were packed into the ship's hold as cargo with little or no room to move.

The arguments against abolition

Those people who owned slaves argued that the economies of Britain's Caribbean colonies would be ruined without slave labour and that the United Kingdom's economy would be damaged by abolition.

Tens of thousands of people were employed either in the slave trade directly or in processing the products of slavery that were brought from the Americas.

Key words

Abolition – getting rid of something, usually a system, practice or organisation.

Abolitionist – someone who supported the abolition of slavery.

Logo – a badge or symbol representing an idea.

MPs – Members of Parliament.

Petitions – very large collections of signatures of people who support an idea.

Pressure groups – groups of people who want to put pressure on governments to change specific laws.

Hints & tips

You must be able to name the leading abolitionists and explain why each was important in the abolition of the slave trade.

All the products produced in the colonies would either not be available in Britain if the slave trade stopped or else they would be much more expensive.

Slave owners said slaves were their property. They would not give up their slaves without government compensation.

Many MPs and members of the House of Lords were slave merchants who did not want to see their wealthy lifestyle put at risk.

There was even a racist argument which claimed that Africans were inferior to Europeans and were not 'real' human beings worth worrying about.

The end of the slave trade

Every year, Wilberforce introduced a bill in the House of Commons to abolish the slave trade. Finally, in 1807 both Houses of Parliament passed Wilberforce's bill. The 1807 Abolition Act made it illegal for any British ships or British people to take part in the slave trade.

However, it did not outlaw slavery itself and people who were already slaves in the Caribbean remained so for a long time afterwards.

Why did the abolitionists win?

The abolition campaign was a grass-roots movement that involved thousands of people. It included ex-slaves such as Olaudah Equiano, social reformers such as Granville Sharp, politicians such as William Wilberforce and passionate abolitionists such as Zachary Macauley.

However, it was not an overnight success. The abolitionist movement took nearly 40 years to reach its goal of ending the trade. Even then it did not end slavery entirely; it took a further 30 years for all slaves in the British Empire to be given their freedom.

Time to reflect !

Find out about modern day pressure/protest groups that interest you. In what ways do the methods used by protest groups now resemble the methods developed by the abolitionist campaigns?

For practice

The following questions are examples of the types of questions you can expect within each of the three parts of the syllabus.

The Atlantic slave trade and the triangular trade

Describe the experience of being captured and held in a 'slave factory' in Africa. (4 marks)
You need to make **four** separate points from recall. You could mention that:

- Africans were often captured by members of other tribes and were sometimes traded into slavery by their own chief
- families were often split up
- slaves often faced a long, forced march to the coast
- they were held in slave factories which were often overcrowded
- branding took place
- they often had a long wait for ships
- slaves became desperate and some even committed suicide.

You can always gain an extra mark if you bring in more information to back up a point you are making. For example: *Africans were often captured by members of other tribes* (1 mark). *This was often the result of being taken as a prisoner during a war between tribes* (1 extra mark). ⇨

Evaluate the usefulness of Source A as evidence of the impact of the triangular trade on Africa. (5 marks)

Source A is an extract from a speech by the Prime Minister, William Pitt, in 1792.

> There is no greater evil than the tearing of 70,000 or 80,000 persons annually from their home land. Slave traders are highly paid to sell these people to us so obviously they will use every method – kidnapping, village breaking, bloodshed and misery – to supply their victims to us. Think about 80,000 persons carried away from their own land. Do you not think of the families left behind?

You need to make **five** clear points about the usefulness of the source.

You would probably start by arguing that the source does provide useful evidence about the impact of triangular trade.

You should comment on who wrote the source, when it was written and why it was written. You must also state why the each of the points you are writing about makes the source useful as evidence. You could mention that:

- the source is a speech by the Prime Minister who would know about the details of the trade
- it was said in 1792 at a time when the triangular trade was booming
- it was said to draw attention to the evils of the trade.

You should then comment on the information contained in the source:

- it describes the effects of the trade on Africans
- it draws attention to the way slaves are captured
- it explains why there is a need for compassion – the separation of families.

However, you could decide that in some ways the source is less useful because of important information that has not been mentioned. For example, it doesn't mention:

- that the trade lasted over 200 years
- that the trade created other problems, e.g. tribal wars fought in order to take prisoners who could be sold as slaves.

The importance of the slave trade to Britain and the Caribbean

Explain the reasons for the success of British ports involved in the slave trade. (6 marks)

You need to give **six** reasons from recall to explain why British ports benefited from the slave trade. You could mention:

- the geographical advantage of ports like Bristol or Liverpool over existing ports like London
- that slave trading was highly profitable
- that wealthy merchants reinvested some of their wealth into their cities
- the rising demand for sugar
- that the trade created employment in other industries
- that these ports grew in size.

You can always gain an extra mark if you bring in more information to back up a point you are making.

For example: *Bristol and Liverpool were successful because of their geographical position* (1 mark). *Being on the west coast gave ships a shorter passage to Africa saving valuable days at sea* (1 extra mark).

Life as a slave and slave resistance

How fully does Source B explain the reasons why it was so difficult for slaves to resist on the middle passage? (6 marks)

Source B is about the way slaves were treated on the middle passage.

> When captured Africans were loaded on board slave ships anchored off the coast they were shocked and disorientated. They had never even seen a sea-going ship before. Who were those people shouting at them, whipping them and forcing them on to the ship? The crew of the slave ship was heavily armed while the captured Africans had neither weapons nor any idea how to sail the ship even if they did manage to take control.

It is a good idea to introduce your answer by saying that the source explains the situation fairly well. This allows you to go on to show what **is** and what **is not** in the source.

You can support this introduction by saying the source mentions that:

- slaves were shocked and disoriented
- the crew were heavily armed
- slaves had no weapons.

However, the source does not mention important points such as:

- slaves were kept below deck
- they were chained up most of the time
- they were often weak due to hunger or disease.

The abolitionist campaigns to end slavery

Explain the reasons for the abolition of the slave trade in 1807. (6 marks)

You need to make **six** separate points from recall. You could mention:

- the abolitionist campaigns, e.g. Clarkson's speaking tours
- that the abolition movement gained important supporters, such as William Pitt
- that many religious people were won over by the moral argument
- other investment opportunities for British entrepreneurs which were more profitable
- sugar production from India
- the effects of the war with France.

You can always gain an extra mark if you bring in more information to back up a point you are making.

For example: *The trade was abolished due to the abolitionist campaigns* (1 mark). *For example, Thomas Clarkson toured the country showing articles he had taken from slaveships* (1 extra mark).

Chapter 6

Changing Britain, 1760–1914

Health and housing – living conditions in Britain, 1760–1914

The first part of the syllabus is about changes in living conditions in Britain between 1760 and 1900, especially changes in health and housing.

What you should know

To be successful in this section you must be able to:
★ explain why problems of overcrowding and poor quality housing led to bad health
★ describe the improvements that were made to housing and water supply in cities
★ explain how the improvements in medicine, water supply and housing up to 1900 led to better public health.

Growing towns and cities

By 1914 Britain had become an urbanised society, with more than half its population living in towns and cities, some of which had hardly existed in 1760.

During the 1800s the Industrial Revolution spread throughout Britain. The use of steam-powered machines led to a massive increase in the number of factories.

As the number of factories grew, people from the countryside began to move into the towns looking for better paid work. These new workers were needed to work the machines and the factory owners built houses for them.

Industrial towns did not have enough rooms or lodgings for the thousands who crowded into them. Rooms were rented to whole families or perhaps several families.

Bad housing and bad health

Most of the new towns were dirty and unhealthy. As towns and cities exploded in size there was no town planning. Basic needs such as clean water and effective sewers to take away human waste were not provided. Pollution was a major problem and living conditions like these were a perfect breeding ground for diseases.

There was not yet an understanding of the link between bad water, overcrowding and bad health.

In 1832 a new disease in Britain called cholera killed more than 31,000 people. Cholera was not the only killer disease. Other diseases, such as

Key words

Cholera – an infectious and deadly disease unknown in Britain before the 1830s and for which there was no cure.

Local authorities – A local council elected by local people who look after what goes on in a town.

Pollution – something introduced to the environment that harms or poisons it.

Public health – the health of the people in a town or city.

Slums – very bad quality housing that often caused poor health.

Urbanised – places that changed from being countryside to towns.

typhus, smallpox and dysentery also killed many people. However, the common causes were bad water, overcrowding and poor diet.

Doctors began to suspect that dirty drinking water was a major cause of disease, but improving public health cost money. Sewers, reservoirs and drains all had to be built but the wealthier people in a town objected to paying for improvements. However, when killer diseases were seen to be killing the rich as well as the poor, these objections stopped.

Gradually, improvements to health and housing were made:
- In 1848, parliament passed laws that allowed city councils to clean up the streets.
- Outside cities, big reservoirs were built and pipes laid to bring fresh water to cities.
- Streets were paved and lighting was put up.
- Drains and sewers were built to take waste away and slowly flush toilets began to appear in people's houses and public lavatories.

By the late nineteenth century, slum clearance was starting. Yet there were still problems. Where would people who lived in slums go to when they were made homeless? New properties could be built but landlords wanted to charge higher rent, which would still leave the poor homeless.

One answer lay in council houses. Local authorities bought land, built houses and charged fair rents to tenants. As the idea spread, council housing estates grew up around cities. People affected by slum clearance in the inner cities moved to the edges of cities to live in brighter, healthier housing.

> ## Time to reflect !
> Do you think the wealthy have a responsibility to help the poor in terms of public health and living conditions generally?

Textiles and coal – changes to working conditions in Britain, 1760–1914

The second part of the syllabus is about changes in working conditions in Britain between 1760 and 1914, especially changes in textile factories and coal mining.

> ## What you should know
> To be successful in this section you must be able to:
> ★ describe working conditions in coal mines and cotton factories around 1800
> ★ explain why working conditions were so dangerous in mills and mines
> ★ describe the improvements that took place in mills and mines because of technological improvements up to 1914
> ★ describe the improvements that took place in mills and mines because of changes in the law up to 1914.

> ## Key words
> **A pit –** a coal mine.
> **Factory –** a large building containing many machines operated by many people.
> **Mill –** usually in the nineteenth century a factory for making textiles such as cotton cloth.
> **Textiles –** any type of cloth, usually at this time cotton or wool.

Cotton mills

By the end of the eighteenth century, cotton cloth was being made in factories.

Cotton cloth was hugely popular. It was light to wear and easy to wash and dry. By the early 1800s, steam power was used to power machines for both spinning and weaving. Factories and mills continued to spread and soaked up tens of thousands of men, women and children looking for work. Many factory workers were children. They worked long hours and sometimes started work as young as four or five years old.

Inside the factory the noise of machines was deafening and the heat often suffocating. Fingers, hair and clothing often got trapped in the machines, leading to severe injuries or death. Discipline was tough and there were few breaks. This went on day after day with only Sundays as a day off and no holidays. Eventually, conditions grew so bad that some people demanded laws to improve working conditions in the mills.

The Factory Acts were a series of laws passed by parliament to limit the number of hours worked by women and children in the textile industry. Men were expected to look after themselves.

At first, factory owners found ways of getting round the new rules. For example, the Factory Act of 1802 reduced working hours yet there were no inspectors to see that owners obeyed the new rules.

In 1833 a new Factory Act stated that:
- Children (aged fourteen to eighteen) must not work more than twelve hours a day without an hour lunch break.
- Children (aged nine to thirteen) must not work more than eight hours without an hour lunch break.
- Children (aged nine to thirteen) must have two hours of education per day.
- Children under nine must not work in the textile factories.

Four inspectors were given the job of enforcing the new law but there were thousands of factories!

The Factory Act of 1844 was the first law to try to make machinery safer. For the first time machinery had to be fenced in and accidental deaths were to be investigated.

Women and young people now worked the same number of hours: no more than twelve hours a day during the week, including one and a half hours for meals, and nine hours on Sundays.

Other Factory Acts followed and by 1878 children under ten had to go to school and could not work in mills. Ten to fourteen year olds could only be employed for half days and women were to work no more than 56 hours per week.

Coal

Coal was the fuel of the Industrial Revolution but coal mines were dangerous places where roofs sometimes caved in, explosions happened and workers got all sorts of injuries. There were very few safety rules.

Time to reflect !

Think about what working for twelve hours a day would mean. Now you are working at school for no more than six or seven hours and that includes breaks and time moving between classes. You only attend five days a week and have about twelve week's holiday a year. Then there were no holidays and only Sunday was not a working day. What effect would working in mills have on your life, what you could do and could not do? How would it affect you? Think widely!

Before 1842, men, women and children worked down a pit. There were four different types of jobs:

- **Hewers** were the men who cut the coal, lying on their backs cutting coal with a pick axe and shovel. The work was very hard and dangerous. Many hewers were killed by rock-falls.
- **Bearers** were women and children who carried coal to the surface, often climbing slippery wooden ladders. The work was heavy, dangerous and exhausting.
- **Trappers** were young children who opened and closed trapdoors in the tunnels in order to make some draughts to help ventilation. Some trappers were only five or six years old. They worked twelve hours each day.
- **Putters** were also young children who filled the tubs and baskets with coal and pushed them to the bottom of the mine shaft. Bearers then carried the basket to the surface.

There were many dangers in coal mines.

- Miners were lowered down on ropes. The ropes could snap or the turning handle could slip and miners would fall to their death.
- In some pits coal was carried up rotting slippery wooden steps.
- If a pit flooded, miners could drown.
- Choke damp was an invisible gas that could suffocate miners.
- Roof falls could trap and kill miners.
- Fire damp was a gas in mines that could cause big explosions.

Later in the nineteenth century new safety laws plus advances in technology led to improvements in mining. However, although coal mining became safer, it was never safe. Some of the safety improvements were:

- a lamp invented by Sir Humphrey Davy, which helped to prevent explosions
- better steam pumps to get water out of the mine
- wire cables to raise and lower cages
- men and equipment were now lowered in iron cages
- efficient ventilation
- steel and iron pit props
- steam engines powering all lifting and lowering machinery
- coal-cutting machinery (although this produced dust that caused illnesses and death).

New laws were also passed to limit working hours for women and children.

The government set up an investigation into working conditions in coal mines in the early 1840s. People were shocked by the report. The result was the Mines Act of 1842.

Sir Humphrey Davy testing his lamp in a mine.

The Mines Act of 1842:

- No woman or child was allowed to work underground.
- Women could work above ground.
- Four inspectors were to inspect all the mines in Britain.
- Ponies were to drag the coal underground.
- No woman or child under fifteen was to work the winding wheel that pulled people and coal back up to the surface.

The Coal Mines Inspection Act and The Coal Mines Regulation Act of 1860 improved safety rules and raised the age limit for boys from ten to twelve.

Other Acts created more inspectors and reduced the working day for miners.

By 1914 coal mines were safer than they had been 100 years before but over 1000 lives were still being lost in mining accidents each year.

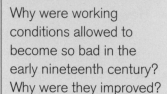

Time to reflect

Why were working conditions allowed to become so bad in the early nineteenth century? Why were they improved?

Remember, this is a 'why' question, so just stating 'laws were passed' will not help because that answers a 'how' question. A 'why' question means you must explain your answer with reasons.

Canals and railways – transport changes in Britain, 1760–1914

The third part of the syllabus is about changes in transport in Britain between 1760 and 1914, especially changes in canals and railways.

What you should know

To be successful in this section you must be able to:

★ describe the building of railways and how Britain quickly became covered in a network of railway lines
★ explain why railways had such a positive effect on society and the economy
★ describe some of the effects of railways on the lives of people in Britain
★ describe how railways affected industry and the economy
★ explain why railways caused the decline of canal and road transport.

Key words

Fragile – easily broken.
Navvies – labourers who built the canals and railways.
'Railway mania' – the same as canal mania but for railways.
Suburbs – the outskirts of a town, usually with more open space and greenery.

Canals

The biggest problem of the early Industrial Revolution was how to carry heavy, bulky items, such as iron and coal and also fragile things, such as pottery goods. Roads simply were not suitable. They were slow, dangerous and full of potholes.

The first answer to Britain's transport problem was canals. It was far easier to pull heavy loads on barges pulled by horses along 'water motorways'. Canals spread across parts of Britain in the eighteenth century but they were not the answer to all transport problems.

Railways

By the 1830s railways replaced canals. Railways had been used for a long time in a very basic way. The earliest railways were simple wagons on wooden rails used to carry coal short distances downhill to rivers or coasts. By 1810 there were about 300 miles of such 'trackways'.

In 1825 the first modern railway began using a locomotive (a moving steam engine), travelling between Stockton and Darlington in the north of England. The railway was used to pull coal wagons.

Five years later in 1830 a railway line carrying passengers between Manchester and Liverpool opened. In Scotland the Garnkirk railway line carried iron, stone and coal around west central Scotland.

Britain was transformed. Within the next twenty years gangs of navvies worked across Britain building a network of rail lines connecting Britain's towns and industrial areas. By the end of the nineteenth century almost every village in Britain was connected.

At first there was some opposition to railways. Some landowners objected to their land being 'invaded' by machines and 'common people'. People complained at the damage to the rural environment and also claimed that animals were scared. Some people were afraid of navvies, the rough, tough builders of railways who were often 'fighting drunk'. Finally, canal operators and coach owners resented the competition from railways which led to unemployment.

Those who were against railways were soon ignored when their benefits became obvious.

- Railways provided a safer, faster and better means of transport around Britain.
- Railways provided thousands of new jobs, from the navvies who created the rail routes, building the bridges and tunnels, to the designers of stations, ticket collectors and train drivers.
- There was a huge demand for iron, coal, timber, glass and leather (to build railways and railway stations).
- News travelled more quickly, with newspapers delivered 'next day' all over the country.
- A national postal service was created as mail could be transported all over the country.
- Towns grew in size as people could travel to work from the suburbs.
- People could afford to go to new seaside holiday resorts, such as North Berwick and Blackpool.
- Food was cheaper and fresher as it could be delivered quickly to towns. A more mixed diet led to better health.
- National political parties grew up with genuinely national policies.
- Remote areas of Britain, such as the Highlands of Scotland, were opened up to tourism.

Time to reflect !

What you have read about was a transport and also a communications revolution. In what ways can it be said we are living in a communications revolution now? Who are the winners and losers in this revolution?

The demand for political change in Britain up to 1867

The fourth part of the syllabus is about the increasing pressure for political change in Britain up to 1867.

What you should know

To be successful in this section you must be able to:

★ explain what is meant by the words 'franchise' and 'democracy'
★ describe how the 1832 Reform Act affected both the franchise and democracy in Britain after 1832
★ explain who the Chartists were and what they wanted
★ make a decision about how effective the campaign of the Chartists was
★ explain why parliament passed the Second Reform Act of 1867
★ describe how the Second Reform Act affected both the franchise and democracy in Britain after 1867.

Radicals protest

In 1815, the war against France, which had lasted for more than twenty years, ended. Thousands of ex-soldiers and sailors returned home to find that there was no work. Across Britain, groups of people who felt unfairly treated began to protest. These protestors were called Radicals. They wanted a fairer society and a change in the basic ways that Britain was run.

The government was worried by Radical protests. They remembered how the French Revolution had started with demands for political reform. The government therefore saw these protests as a dangerous threat that should be stopped.

Peterloo

On Sunday 16 August 1819 a large meeting of Radicals was held at St Peter's Fields, Manchester. Men, women and children hoped to hear speeches asking for political reform.

As the crowd grew in size to about 20,000, the authorities grew worried. No one is quite sure what happened next, but the yeomanry moved into the crowd. When the demonstration was cleared eleven people lay dead and 200 were wounded, many with blood streaming from their heads.

The event was later called the Peterloo Massacre. Four years earlier the British cavalry had helped win the final battle against the French at Waterloo. At St Peter's Fields, the name Peterloo was a sarcastic condemnation of the cowardly attack by yeomanry on a peaceful demonstration.

Key words

Bribery – giving gifts of money or food and drink to persuade people to vote as they were told.

Electoral districts – areas that sent an MP to parliament. Another term for an electoral district is a 'constituency'.

Radicals – people who supported political reform.

Redistributing seats – removing the right to send an MP to parliament from an area where fewer people lived and giving that right to an area that had become more populated.

Rotten boroughs – electoral areas under the control of a local landowner who chose the MP.

Transported – a punishment used to get rid of troublemakers. They were sent to prison camps in Australia and not expected to ever return.

Whig – an old name for the Liberal Party.

Yeomanry – a local group of mounted part-time soldiers who were used to stop radical protests.

The Reform Act of 1832

By 1830 Britain had a new Whig government and fears of a violent revolution in Britain were fading.

At the time, there were two political parties in Britain: the Whigs and the Tories. The Whigs hoped that, by giving some power to the wealthier middle classes, pressure for more reform would be decreased and the Radicals would lose support.

The Great Reform Act of 1832 gave the vote to some men who owned or rented property up to a certain value. Some rotten boroughs lost the right to send MPs to parliament because almost no one lived there anymore. The Act also got rid of many confusing and differing rules about who could vote depending on where people lived.

After all the fuss, the Great Reform Act of 1832 still meant that five out of six adult men could not vote and no women could vote at all. Those men who could vote still had to vote in public, meaning that threats and bribery were still common.

The Great Reform Act left many working-class people bitterly disappointed.

The Chartists

The Chartist movement was born out of the disappointment with the Reform Act of 1832.

In 1836, the London Working Men's Association was formed. It wanted much greater political reform, especially reforms to give the working classes real influence in the government.

The Chartists had six demands:
- Universal manhood suffrage – all men should have the vote.
- Secret voting.
- Equal electoral districts, so that each MP represented roughly the same number of people.
- Elections every year so that MPs could be voted out if they did not keep their promises.
- No property qualification for members of parliament so people who did not own land could become MPs.
- Payment for members of parliament so poor men could afford to become MPs.

These demands were listed on a document called The People's Charter, which is why supporters of these demands were called Chartists.

The Chartists were divided over how they wanted to achieve their target. One leader, William Lovett, believed in peaceful protest, while another leader, Fergus O'Connor, was in favour of more violent protest.

In the short term the Chartists failed but in the longer term, their ideas lived on to inspire other protest groups. In the following 60 years all but one of the Chartist's demands had become reality.

The Second Reform Act of 1867

By the 1860s, pressure for political change was growing again and there was much less opposition to the idea of change. Protest groups such as the Reform League and Reform Union organised large-scale demonstrations across the UK. Politicians also accepted that skilled working men were educated, reasonable people who could be trusted with the vote.

Why 1867?

The answer lies with politicians trying to gain an advantage for their party.

The Liberals (previously known as Whigs) were led by Gladstone and they proposed a Second Reform Act. However, a row then broke out among the Liberals and they lost power. After twenty years out of power the Conservatives (formerly known as Tories) saw their chance.

The new Conservative Prime Minister, Benjamin Disraeli, knew that once the Liberals sorted themselves out then they would soon be back in power and would pass their own Reform Act.

Disraeli acted quickly, stealing the Liberal ideas and claiming the Second Reform Act as a Conservative reform! At the time, Disraeli's actions were called 'stealing the Liberal's clothes'.

What did the 1867 Reform Act do?

Put simply, more men got the right to vote and the voting system was made fairer.

The right to vote was given to skilled working-class men in towns who rented property worth £10 a year in terms of local tax value.

The voting system was also made fairer by redistributing seats. A seat meant a seat in parliament for one MP, so redistribution meant reorganising the areas that sent an MP to parliament. Such an area is called a constituency. The population of Britain was still changing as some industrial towns grew hugely and other places became almost deserted. To make the system fairer, some areas that were depopulated lost the right to choose an MP while extra seats were given to more populated areas.

Did the 1867 Reform Act make Britain democratic?

Democracy means political power is in the hands of the adult population so the short answer is no.

Women still couldn't vote and voting was still done in public, leaving voters open to threats and bullying. Also, the Reform Act did not affect working men in the countryside. There was still a long time to wait for changes that would make Britain truly democratic. Between 1867 and 1914, the following reforms did help to make Britain more democratic.

- 1872 secret voting
- 1884 the vote for skilled men in the countryside
- 1911 the power of the House of Lords was reduced
- 1911 payment for MPs so that any man could try to become a politician

Time to reflect !

There is currently a debate in Scotland about lowering the voting age to sixteen. Do you think it should be lowered to sixteen, and if not, why not? Are the arguments against it not just the same as denying the vote to women and working-class men in the nineteenth century?

For practice

The following questions are examples of the types of questions you can expect within each of the three parts of the syllabus.

Health and housing – living conditions in Britain, 1760–1914

Explain the reasons for poor health in British cities at the start of the nineteenth century. (6 marks)

You need to make **six** separate points from recall. You could mention:

● that the increase in urban population had led to severe overcrowding
● that housing was often built to a poor standard, for example, lacking ventilation or sunlight
● the lack of proper sanitation
● that people in cities often had a poor diet because they could not get fresh milk, fruit and vegetables easily
● that poor city dwellers had limited access to proper medical care
● that poor working conditions often led to ill-health.

You can always gain an extra mark if you bring in more information to back up a point you are making. For example: *One reason for poor health was the increase in the urban population which led to overcrowding* (1 mark). *Whole families would often have to share one or two rooms allowing disease to spread easily* (1 extra mark).

Textiles and coal – changes to working conditions in Britain, 1760–1914

How fully does Source A explain how new technology improved safety in coal mines by 1900? (6 marks)

Source A explains the effects of new technology in coal mines by 1900.

> There were three main dangers in coal mines - flooding, gas explosions and roof collapse. Flooding had been reduced by the use of steam pumps and explosions were made less common by better ventilation thanks to exhaust fans which pushed bad air out of the mine shafts. When Sir Humphrey Davy invented his safety lamp, miners no longer worked long hours lit only by candle light or the glow of rotting fish heads. New technology did help to reduce the dangers of coal mining but the miners were never entirely safe.

It is a good idea to start off by saying that the source explains the situation fairly well. This allows you to go on to say what **is** and what **is not** in the source to support your introductory comment. The source mentions:

● steam pumps reduced the risk of flooding
● better ventilation thanks to exhaust fans which pushed bad air out
● Davy lamps improved lighting.

You should then say that the source does not mention important points such as:

● Davy lamps also reduced danger of explosion
● winding engines and cages made getting to and from the coal face safer
● pit props supported the roofs of the mine.

Evaluate the usefulness of Source B as evidence about working conditions in cotton mills in the nineteenth century. (5 marks)

⇨

Source B was written by a visitor to a cotton mill in Bolton, Lancashire in 1847.

> The workers are well clothed and fed. The mill is a large building and kept very clean. The working rooms were spacious and well ventilated. There were many windows in each room. I observed that great care had been taken to put guards on dangerous machinery. I was told accidents were very rare and were caused by stupidity or negligence by the worker.

You need to make **five** clear points about the usefulness of the source.

You would probably start by arguing that the source does provide useful evidence about working conditions.

You should comment on who wrote the source, when it was written and why it was written. You must also state why each of the points you are writing about makes the source useful as evidence.

You could mention that:

- the author had visited a cotton mill in Bolton
- the source was written in 1847, at a time when some improvements were being made to working conditions
- the source was written to describe working conditions in a cotton mill.

You should also comment on what the source says:

- The source mentions that the factory is very clean.
- The source describes spacious and well ventilated work rooms.
- The source claims that guards on the machinery have reduced accidents.

However, you could decide that in some ways the source is less useful because the author shows bias by blaming all accidents on workers' stupidity and negligence.

You could also decide that in some ways the source is less useful because of important information that has not been mentioned.

- Factory Acts had been introduced to improve working conditions, especially for children.
- Many mill owners did not obey the new regulations.
- Many mills were still dangerous.

Canals and railways – transport in Britain, 1760–1914

Describe the impact of the growth of the railway network on the British economy. (4 marks)

You need to make **four** separate points from recall. You could mention:

- the need for fuel boosted the coal industry
- the need for tracks and locomotives boosted iron industry
- that postal services and communication became quicker and more efficient
- that railways provided cheaper transport of raw materials and manufactured goods
- the boost to employment for railway building
- the decline of canals.

You can always gain an extra mark if you bring in more information to back up a point you are making. For example: *The need for fuel boosted the coal industry* (1 mark). *A reliable supply of fuel was needed for the growing number of steam locomotives* (1 extra mark).

The demand for political change in Britain up to 1867

Compare the views in Source C and Source D on the reasons for the rise of the Chartist movement. (4 marks)

Sources C and **D** discuss the reasons for the rise of Chartism.

Source C

> Working people had believed that the 1832 Reform Act would be a step towards wider democracy. There was anger when the Whig government failed to deliver. Also, wages were falling and there was fury over the new Poor Law which established the workhouse system. An increased demand for revolutionary change in society led to the Chartist movement. Also, after the repeal of some anti-trade union laws, workers were more confident about forming their own organisations.

Source D

> The Great Reform Act gave the vote to male householders who owned property. Many middle-class men benefited. However, still less than a fifth of the population could vote. This caused fury among many working-class people who had expected the vote. Two years later, parliament passed the Poor Law Amendment Act which introduced the hated workhouses. This, combined with the case of the Tolpuddle Martyrs, created a working-class backlash which gave rise to the Chartist movement.

For this type of question you must say whether you think the sources agree or not and then support your decision by making two comparisons using evidence from the sources either by making 4 simple comparisons stating what the sources agree or disagree on, or by supporting your comparison with evidence from the sources – this is called a developed comparison. Two developed comparisons are worth the full 4 marks.

For this question you would probably decide that the two sources agree. You could then back this up with two of the following comparisons:

- Source C mentions working-class anger at the Whig government over the 1832 act. Source D describes working-class fury at continuing restrictions on voting which remained after the act.
- Source C mentions people's anger at the Poor Law and Source D also tells us about the hatred of the laws.
- Source C mentions working-class people being confident about forming their own organisations while Source D mentions a working-class backlash.

You can find out more about the Chartists at www.chartistancestors.co.uk

Chapter 7

The Making of Modern Britain, 1880–1951

A divided society? – British society around 1900

The first part of the syllabus is about British society around 1900.

What you should know

To be successful in this section you must be able to:

★ explain what the phrases 'laissez-faire', 'self-help' and 'deserving poor' mean
★ explain why the Booth and Rowntree reports changed attitudes to poverty and the poor
★ describe the reasons why the Liberal government decided to pass a series of social reforms.

Poverty in the late nineteenth century

Poverty was a huge social problem at the end of the nineteenth century. Many people who were not poor believed that poverty was caused by laziness, drunkenness or personal failure. 'Self-help' was the idea that people should work hard and make sure they did not fall into poverty. Government policy at this time was called laissez-faire. It meant that most people accepted that poverty and hardship were not things the government could or should do anything about.

Booth and Rowntree

By 1900, attitudes to poverty were changing, partly because of two large investigations. In London, Charles Booth provided hard evidence that poverty affected almost 30 per cent of the population. He also claimed that poverty had definite causes that were beyond the ability of an individual to 'self help' themselves out of.

Another investigation was carried out by Seebohm Rowntree in York and it discovered very similar results.

The reports of Charles Booth and Seebohm Rowntree were important for several reasons:
- The reports showed that poverty had causes.
- The reports showed that no matter how hard certain people tried, they could not lift themselves out of poverty.
- The reports provided evidence that self-help could not cure poverty. Causes of poverty such as old age or unemployment were beyond the ability of an individual to solve on their own.

Key words

Deserving poor – those people such as the old and the young who were poor through no fault of their own and who deserved help.

Laissez-faire – a French phrase meaning leave alone. Around 1900, the government did not think it was its responsibility to help the poor.

Poverty – a lack of money that leads to bad housing, bad health, poor education and other social problems.

Self-help – an idea that people should help themselves to get out of poverty through their own hard work.

- Politicians accepted that thousands of people in Britain were poor through no fault of their own and needed help. These people were called the 'deserving poor'. They included children, the old, the sick and the unemployed.

Changing attitudes towards poverty within the Liberal Party

There were several reasons why the Liberal government decided to help the poor.

1 The Liberal government that came to power in 1906 was persuaded by the findings of the Booth and Rowntree reports to take action against poverty.
2 Younger politicians within the Liberal Party were convinced the government should take more direct action to help the poor.
3 The Liberals were concerned that the newly formed Labour Party would promise to offer social reforms if they were elected. The Liberals were therefore worried they would lose votes to Labour.
4 In 1899 Britain fought a war in South Africa. During the war, many volunteers for the army were rejected because they were unfit to fight. Liberal politicians wondered if Britain would be strong enough to fight a bigger and better enemy in the future.
5 Britain needed healthier and better-educated workers. However, many children were thought to be too hungry and badly clothed to learn effectively.

Time to reflect

Do you think government policy towards the poor changed because politicians were genuinely worried about the 'deserving poor' or were there more politically selfish reasons?

Do you think help for the poor should only be given to people who are defined as 'deserving'? What about the 'undeserving'? How would you define the undeserving poor?

The Liberal reforms 1906–14

The second part of the syllabus is about the Liberal reforms between 1906 and 1914.

What you should know

To be successful in this section you must be able to:

★ describe in some detail what the Liberals did to help the old, the young, the sick and the unemployed
★ decide how successful the Liberal reforms were.

The Liberal reforms of 1906–14 were very important because they showed that the government was prepared to help the deserving poor. Between 1906 and 1914 the Liberal reforms focused on four groups: the old, the young, the sick and the unemployed.

The Liberals and the old

In 1908 the Old Age Pensions Act was passed to help those people who were too old to work. A single person over 70 got a pension of 5 shillings (25 pence) a week, while a married couple got 7 shillings and 6 pence (37·5 pence) each week.

Key words

Compulsory – something that must happen.
Contributions – money paid by people towards their own benefits. The government and employers also paid into the total.
Insurance – preparing for future difficulties, usually by paying money regularly towards an insurance policy.

Old-age pensions helped, but they were not the answer to poverty in old age.

Critics of the old-age pension plan argued that the amount paid was too low and that few of the genuinely poor would live until their seventieth birthday so would not benefit.

The Liberals and children

School meals

In 1906 the Liberals passed the Provision of School Meals Act. Local authorities were permitted to raise money by increasing rates (a local tax based on property values), but the law did not force local authorities to provide school meals. School meals did make a difference to the children who received them but not all children did. Children in poor areas gained weight when they attended school but lost weight again during the holidays.

Medical inspections

In 1907, medical inspections for children in school were made compulsory. However, there was no guarantee that each child would be treated. When free medical treatment for school children began in 1912 problems could be dealt with properly.

The Children's Charter

In 1908 a Children's Act banned children under sixteen from smoking, drinking alcohol or begging. New juvenile courts were set up for children accused of committing crimes. Children found guilty of committing crimes were sent to children's prisons called borstals rather than adult prisons.

All these reforms were called the Children's Charter but some parts of the Charter were difficult to enforce, while others took time to put into place.

The Liberals and the unemployed

The National Insurance Act only helped unemployed workers in seven industries. Workers had to pay contributions towards their benefits and so did employers and the government.

The benefit was seven shillings a week, paid for a maximum of fifteen weeks. The benefits were paid at the recently opened labour exchanges. At the labour exchanges, which were similar to today's job centres, workers could more easily find out what jobs were available in their area.

The scheme was useful because it meant newly unemployed workers had fifteen weeks to look for work. The new labour exchanges also made finding new work much easier.

However, because most of Britain's workers were not covered by unemployment insurance they received no help at all.

Key words

One shilling – an amount of money, now worth around 5p. (Be aware that the value of money changes over time. In 1900 the average wage of a working man was about £1 per week. Now it is £500.)

The Liberals and the sick

All wage earners between the ages of sixteen and seventy had to join the health scheme. The scheme was called a contributory system, as each worker paid four pence a week towards the help they received. The employer paid three pence a week for each employee and the government paid two pence a week. That meant each insured worker got nine pence in benefits each week but only paid four pence themselves. The plan was soon called 'ninepence for fourpence'.

Any money coming in as 'sick pay insurance benefit' would help a family during hard times, but the new law only helped a bit.

- Firstly, only the insured worker got free medical treatment from a doctor. Other family members did not benefit from the scheme.
- Secondly, the scheme did not apply to the self-employed or the slightly better paid.
- Thirdly, the insurance did not cover hospital treatment or treatment by dentists or opticians.
- Finally, the benefits themselves were very low and they stopped after 26 weeks.

How effective were the Liberal reforms in helping the poor?

The National Insurance Act is a good illustration of the change in government policy in the early twentieth century. The government was prepared to intervene to help the poor, but as part of the deal the poor also had to help themselves by paying contributions towards their benefits.

The Liberal reforms of 1906–14 are very important because they marked the decline of the laissez-faire ideology and the acceptance of the idea that the government should have a large part to play in helping those who could not help themselves.

> **Time to reflect**
>
> The Liberal reforms are described as a halfway-house between a welfare state (see page 64) and laissez-faire. Winston Churchill (a Liberal politician) said the reforms were like a lifebelt thrown to a struggling swimmer. The reforms were not meant to drag him to shore but would allow him to help himself by swimming ashore. What do you think Churchill meant?

How World War Two affected life in Britain

The third part of the syllabus is about how the Second World War affected life in Britain.

> **What you should know**
>
> To be successful in this section you must be able to:
> - ★ describe what is meant by bombing, rationing and evacuation
> - ★ explain how wartime experiences such as bombing, rationing and evacuation had an effect on attitudes to poverty
> - ★ describe how the Beveridge Report helped to make clear what the main social problems in Britain were.

> **Key words**
>
> **Beveridge Report** – a report about social conditions that identified five main problems. Written by Sir William Beveridge in 1942.

Government intervention during World War Two

The Second World War was important in making people more willing to accept greater government intervention. The phrase 'post-war must be better than pre-war' sums up public attitudes during the war. It meant that people wanted a better Britain after the war.

During the war, the government organised the rationing of food, clothing and fuel and gave extra milk and meals for expectant mothers and children. Free hospital treatment for war wounds – including treatment for civilians with bomb injuries – and free immunisation are both examples of the move towards a free health service. And the public got used to higher levels of taxation to pay for these services.

Bombing

During the war, Britain's main cities and ports were bombed by the German airforce. By the end of the war large areas of inner cities were destroyed. Post-war there was an opportunity for town planners to redesign city centres and build better housing.

Rationing

During the war the government organised the rationing of food to make sure people got fair shares of food and to prevent prices rocketing as supplies were reduced. Rationing also prepared the public for greater government control in their lives. People were told to register with local shops and given ration cards. The shops were given enough supplies to meet the needs of their customers. People had to plan their shopping based on the ration cards that they could use that week.

Evacuation

Just before the war started thousands of children were evacuated from danger zones such as big cities and ports. Many of these children were very poor and when they arrived in more middle-class areas, the host families were shocked to see just how poor the children were. Many had lice or skin diseases and suffered from malnutrition. People were surprised to see that such poverty still existed in Britain.

The Beveridge Report

The war government commissioned an investigation on social insurance in Britain. The result was a report written in 1942 by Sir William Beveridge. It was not expected to cause much interest. Instead, the report became a bestseller and provided a model of what a new welfare system could look like. It also provided hope for how to improve British society after the war was won.

Evacuation – sending children away from areas that were at high risk of being bombed.

Evacuees – children who were evacuated.

Government intervention – the government got involved in helping people cope with problems that before the war people would have had to deal with themselves.

Post-war – after the war ended.

Pre-war – before the war started.

Rationing – controlling supplies of many things such as food, clothing and fuel to cope with shortages caused by the war.

Sir William Beveridge

The Beveridge Report identified five giant social problems affecting Britain:

- Want
- Disease
- Idleness
- Ignorance
- Squalor.

In other words, the problems were poverty, illness, unemployment, poor education and bad housing.

The Labour government and the welfare state, 1945–1951

The fourth part of the syllabus is about how the Labour government tried to create a welfare state in Britain between 1945 and 1951.

What you should know

To be successful in this section you must be able to:

★ describe how the Labour government of 1945 tried to deal with each of the 'five giants'
★ explain what is meant by a welfare state that looks after people 'from the cradle to the grave'
★ make a decision about how successful each of the reforms were.

Key words

Idleness – unemployment.
Ignorance – poor education.
Squalor – bad housing.
Want – poverty.
Welfare state – the government (or state) looking after the well-being (welfare) of all the people in the country.

The welfare state

Between 1945 and 1951, the Labour government introduced many social reforms that tried to help improve the lives of the British people.

Those social reforms were the foundation of what we now call the welfare state. In a welfare state, the government provides a safety net of support through which no one should fall into poverty. The core idea of the welfare state is that everyone can receive help if and when they need it throughout their life – in other words, 'from the cradle to the grave'.

The Labour government's reforms were aimed at defeating each of the social problems – the five giants listed by Beveridge.

Want

The new National Insurance Act of 1946 provided improved sickness and unemployment benefit, old-age pensions for women at sixty and men at sixty-five, widows' and orphans' pensions and maternity and death grants.

A Family Allowance Act (1945) was also passed to help mothers look after their families if they had two or more children.

The National Assistance Act (1948) helped people who were not in work or the old who had not paid enough contributions into the new National Insurance scheme. People in need could apply for help from National Assistance Boards.

Finally, an Industrial Injuries Act (1946) paid compensation for all injuries caused at work.

By including all workers and families in the scheme, it seemed the benefit system would be very helpful.

However, weekly payments into the insurance fund took up about five per cent of average earnings. People joining the insurance scheme for the first time did not get full pension benefits for ten years and the pensions themselves were still not enough to live on.

Disease

In 1948 the Labour government created a National Health Service (NHS) that was based on three main aims:
- it was for everybody
- it would treat all medical problems
- no patient would be asked to pay for any treatment at the point of access.

The biggest difficulty with the NHS was its huge cost. Demand for NHS services surprised everyone. The extent of ill health among the population had not been realised. The running expenses of the NHS were reduced slightly by charging a small amount of money for false teeth, spectacles and prescriptions. Some Labour politicians resigned in protest at this, saying it was breaking the main idea of 'free at the point of need'.

Squalor

Labour promised homes for everyone and aimed to build 200,000 houses each year. Most of the new houses were council houses for rent. Many were prefabricated houses – 'prefabs' for short – which were made in factories in sections and quickly assembled on site.

Cities became encircled with new council housing estates. In many ways, council estates were a big improvement in people's living conditions. They offered a brighter and healthier future for people who had been living in overcrowded tenements in the centre of the cities.

The New Towns Act of 1946 planned for the building of fourteen new towns, including Glenrothes and East Kilbride. These were to be 'people-friendly' towns that aimed to relieve the housing problems in older cities.

In spite of the huge number of houses built by the Labour government, there was still a serious housing shortage in 1951 and long waiting lists for council housing.

Ignorance

Before 1939, many children received no education after primary school. Beveridge wanted a free education system that would allow working-class children with ability to gain a good education.

The Education Act of 1944 raised the school leaving age to fifteen.

An exam at the age of eleven (called the 'eleven-plus' exam, or the 'qualy' – short for the Qualification Exam – in Scotland) placed children in certain types of school according to ability.

For those who passed the 11+ exam, the system worked well. However, those children who failed the exam seemed to be stuck in a trap of low expectations and inferior education. Many people were against the idea of deciding a child's future at the age of eleven or twelve.

Idleness

After the war, the Labour government wanted to avoid high unemployment.

Labour's answer to the problem of unemployment was nationalisation. Nationalisation meant that the government would take over major industries to control the economy and make sure people had jobs. However, nationalisation was costly and at times led to bad management.

How successful were the Labour government's reforms, 1945–1951?

The Beveridge Report provided hope to war-weary people who wanted to believe that post-war Britain would be a land worth fighting for. Labour's reforms went a long way to creating a post-war Britain based on ideas of fairness and help for all who needed it.

By 1951, for the first time ever, the government had removed worries of how to cope with unemployment and serious illness and a start had been made in providing decent housing and education for everyone. The Labour government had tried to build a fair society, where help was available to all.

Time to reflect !

Did the Labour welfare reforms finally replace old laissez-faire and self-help attitudes?

For practice

The following questions are examples of the types of questions you can expect within each of the three parts of the syllabus.

A divided society? – British society around 1900

How fully does Source A explain the reasons why attitudes to the poor began to change by the start of the 20th century? (6 marks)

Source A is about changing attitudes to poverty at the start of the 20th century.

> By 1900 many people were concerned by the evidence of extreme poverty across Britain. Socialist groups campaigned to improve living conditions, but it was the reports of Booth and Rowntree - in London and York - that helped to convince Liberal politicians of the need to take action to help the poor. The Liberals were already embarrassed to see Germany providing improvements to the living and working conditions of its working people. Why could Britain not do the same?

It is a good idea to introduce your answer by saying that the source explains the situation fairly well. This allows you to go on to show what **is** and what **is not** in the source.

You can support this introduction by saying the source mentions that:

- new political groups campaigned for improved living conditions
- Booth and Rowntree reports showed that action on poverty was needed
- the Liberals were embarrassed by improvements made in the lives of working people in Germany.

However, the source does not mention important points such as:

- young 'new liberals' argued that the government must do more to tackle poverty
- army recruitment during the Boer war had shown poor health among working-class males
- British industry was struggling to compete with other countries due to the poor state of British workers.

The Liberal reforms 1906–14

Describe the impact of the Liberal reforms on working people. (4 marks)

You need to make **four** separate points from recall. You could mention that:

- the National Insurance scheme provided sickness benefits
- some workers could claim unemployment benefits through National Insurance
- labour exchanges were set up to help people find jobs
- Workers' Compensation Act entitled many workers to claim compensation for injuries at work
- the eight-hour working day was established for miners
- working hours for shop assistants were reduced
- old-age pensions meant that there was less pressure to save for old age and workers could stop work at 70 and still receive an income
- less of parents' income had to be spent on feeding their children thanks to free school meals.

You can always gain an extra mark if you bring in more information to back up a point you are making.

For example: *The introduction of a National Insurance scheme provided sickness benefits* (1 mark). *A working man who had paid contributions could claim sick pay if he was unable to work due to ill-health* (1 extra mark).

$\Rightarrow$

Compare the views in Sources B and C as evidence about the impact of the Liberal reforms. (4 marks)

Sources B and **C** describe the impact of the Liberal social reforms.

Source B

> The Liberal social reforms were not introduced to help bring about a welfare state. They were not intended as a comprehensive system of welfare provision. Rather, they involved targeting certain small areas of the problem of poverty. It meant that those who were not included continued to need a safety net. The poor law was less important but it would still be necessary for some people.

Source C

> All the Liberal reforms offered levels of support that were only designed to support the poor but not to free them from poverty. The new measures helped to insure certain types of workers against sickness and unemployment. It was true that some people were freed from having to seek poor relief but living on 5 shillings a week in old age was almost impossible.

For this type of question you must say whether you think the sources agree or not . You can make 4 simple comparisons stating what the sources agree or disagree on or you can support your comparison with evidence from the sources – this is called a developed comparison. Two developed comparisons are worth the full 4 marks.

You will probably decide that the two sources agree. You could then back this up with two of the following comparisons.

- Source B says that the reforms were in no sense a welfare state and Source C says that reforms were not designed to free people from poverty.
- Source B says that the reforms targeted small areas of poverty and Source C mentions that only certain types of worker were supported for sickness and unemployment.
- Source B says that the poor law was still necessary and Source C says that only some people were freed from having to seek poor relief.

How World War Two affected life in Britain

To what extent was the experience of rationing important in changing attitudes to poverty by 1945? (9 marks)

Write a short introduction showing you understand there were other factors which contributed to changing attitudes to poverty by 1945. List these factors in your introduction.

You should then explain why rationing was important. You could mention:

- rationing was introduced by the government to try to ensure that food was distributed equally to everyone.
- the government was stepping in to make sure that poor people were not deprived of food because of rising prices.
- many people thought that this kind of intervention by the government was fair.

You should then balance your answer by giving other important reasons for changing attitudes to poverty:

- many people agreed with government support for victims of bombing.
- evacuation made more middle-class people aware of the effects of poverty.

- the war brought a desire for a fairer society after the war.
- many people supported or were influenced by the Beveridge Report of 1942.

You should finish with a conclusion that gives an overall answer to the question and support it with a reason for the judgement you have made.

For example: *Overall, the experience of rationing was very important in changing attitudes to poverty because most people believed it was fair that the government rationed the food available.*

Evaluate the usefulness of Source D as evidence of the attitudes towards welfare reform after the Second World War. (5 marks)

Source D is taken from a speech made by Winston Churchill before the 1945 election.

> Here in old England we do not like to have every aspect of our lives organised for us. Let us leave Labour's welfare reformers to their unrealistic dreams. Let us make sure that the home to which the soldiers return is blessed with modest but solid prosperity but that Britons remain free to plan their lives for themselves and for those they love.

You need to make **five** clear points about the usefulness of the source.

You would probably start by arguing that the source does provide useful evidence about attitudes to the welfare state after the Second World War.

You should comment on who wrote the source, when it was written and why it was written. You must also state why each of the points you are writing about makes the source useful as evidence. You could mention that:

- the author was Prime Minister at the beginning of 1945 and would know about welfare reform
- the source comes from a speech made at a time when welfare reform was being debated
- it was written to explain why welfare reform was not necessary.

You should also comment on what the source says:

- the source tells us that Labour reformers were unrealistic dreamers
- it mentions that there was a need for solid prosperity
- it says that British people should be free to plan their own lives.

You could decide however that in some ways the source is less useful because:

- Churchill was campaigning against Labour's plans for reform so he could possibly be biased
- his party was heavily defeated in the election, which suggests that his views were not widely supported.

You could also decide that in some ways the source is less useful because of important information that has not been mentioned.

- Many British people supported the idea of welfare reform.
- The Beveridge Report was very popular in Britain and sold thousands of copies.

The Labour government and the welfare state, 1945–51

Explain the reasons why the Labour government introduced a programme of welfare reform between 1945 and 1951. (6 marks)

You need to make **six** separate points from recall. You could mention that:

- British people had come to expect the government would provide welfare for those in need during the war e.g. rationing
- the Beveridge Report had provided a plan for tackling Britain's social problems through government welfare provision
- Labour won the 1945 election after promising welfare reform

⇒

- the experience of war had led people to support the building of a fairer society in the future
- memories of the hardships of the 1930s were still strong
- the lack of schools and teachers, along with inaccessible healthcare and an inadequate system of National Insurance plus the desire not to return to the high unemployment and housing shortages of the 1930s.

You can always gain an extra mark if you bring in more information to back up a point you are making.

For example: *Welfare reforms were introduced because British people had come to expect the government to provide welfare for those in need* (1 mark). *Rationing ensured that even the poorest gained a share of scarce food supplies* (1 extra mark).

Describe the impact of Labour's reforms on the young. (4 marks)

You need to make **four** separate points from recall. You could mention:

- the effects of the Education Act – free secondary education for all, the new types of school, and the raising of the school leaving age
- the effects of the Family Allowance Act – reduced child poverty
- the effects of the NHS – free health care, reduced child mortality and improved health
- the effects of Housing Acts – fewer children living in overcrowded housing
- that problems still remained e.g. school building/hospital building/housing projects were delayed.

You can always gain an extra mark if you bring in more information to back up a point you are making.

For example: *Labour introduced the Education Act giving free secondary education to all children* (1 mark). *Previously, most secondary education had to be paid for by parents through school fees* (1 extra mark).

Chapter 8

Hitler and Nazi Germany, 1919–1939

Weimar Germany, 1919–1929

The first part of the syllabus is about Germany under the Weimar Government between 1919 and 1929.

What you should know

To be successful in this section you must be able to:
★ describe what happened in Germany in November 1918 and include the words 'monarchy', 'revolution', 'abdicate' and 'republic'
★ describe how Germany was affected by the Treaty of Versailles
★ describe the good and bad points of the Weimar constitution
★ describe the economic crisis of 1923 and its effects
★ describe the main events of the Munich Putsch and its results.

The end of the First World War

By the late summer of 1918 the German people were physically and emotionally exhausted. Coal was in short supply and this led to power cuts. Rationing further reduced food that was already scarce. People searched in fields and gutters for scraps of rotting food.

German citizens were desperate. The people were starving, soldiers were having their wounds wrapped in paper and thousands of soldiers were deserting. Thousands of people died when a flu epidemic raced through the country. To make things worse, America had recently joined the war against Germany and in August 1918, a huge allied offensive completely broke the German army's strength.

In early 1918 President Wilson of the USA had offered Germany a fourteen-point peace plan, but the German military leaders rejected Wilson's offer because they hoped to win the war. By November 1918 attitudes against Germany had hardened. The allied leaders wanted to put the Kaiser on trial for war crimes and there was even a demand to 'Hang the Kaiser'.

At the end of October 1918 discipline in the German navy cracked. A mutiny is when soldiers or sailors refuse to follow orders and this exactly what happened at the German naval base of Kiel on 3 November 1918.

The mutiny at Kiel sparked off other mutinies and by 6 November groups of soldiers and workers were in power in the ports of Hamburg, Bremen and Lubeck. The soldiers and sailors had formed 'workers' councils' to govern their local areas. They had copied their ideas from Russia where there had been a revolution a few months before.

The revolution spread quickly so that by 9 November, workers' and soldiers' councils even ruled in the German capital city, Berlin.

Key words

Abdicate – to give up power or resign.
Constitution – the basic rules that govern a country.
Democracy – political power in the hands of the people.
Hyperinflation – collapse in the value of money.
Kaiser – the ruler of Germany before 1918.
Putsch – an attempt to overthrow the government.
Spartacists – German communists who wanted a revolution in Germany.
Weimar Germany – the name given to the German government between 1919 and 1933.

The Kaiser's closest advisers finally convinced him to give up his throne. On 9 November it was announced that the Kaiser had abdicated. On 10 November the Kaiser left Germany by train for the Netherlands and on 11 November an armistice was signed. The war was over.

A new provisional government was created in Germany, led by Friedrich Ebert, leader of the Social Democratic Party (SPD). At the same time the Spartacists, who later became known as the Communist Party or KPD, tried to start a revolution to create a new communist Germany. The attempted revolution failed. Ebert had help from the army and groups of ex-soldiers called Freikorps to destroy the revolutionaries.

The Weimar constitution

The title 'Weimar Germany' or 'The Weimar Republic' refers to a time between 1919 and 1933 when Germany was a republic ruled by elected representatives. The new democratic republic was created in the town of Weimar because it was peaceful and far from the street violence of Berlin. There, a set of rules about how Germany was to be governed was written. The rules were called a constitution and it tried to be fair to everyone. However, the new Weimar constitution also had serious weaknesses.

The Treaty of Versailles

Why were so many Germans against the Treaty of Versailles?

The victorious allies wanted to make sure that Germany was never a threat to European peace again. To achieve this they first had to make Germany a much weaker country.

On 28 June 1919, Germany signed the Treaty of Versailles which officially ended the Great War. German politicians had hoped that as Germany was now a democratic republic, they would have a say in negotiating a fair treaty. They were wrong. Under the Treaty of Versailles Germany was not only punished, it was humiliated:

- Germany's military power was reduced.
- Germany had to give away part of its territory.
- All German colonies were taken from Germany by the victorious allies.
- Germany was forced to accept full responsibility for causing ALL of the deaths and damage done during the war. That part of the Treaty was called the **war guilt clause**.

Of course, once Germany had 'accepted' that they were guilty of causing the war, it was only natural to insist that Germany paid compensation for the war they caused. As a result, the allies insisted that Germany would have to pay compensation to the allies. The word used for compensation was **reparations**.

Many Germans believed that Germany had not really been defeated. They rightly pointed out that the country had not been invaded and

Chapter 9

Red Flag: Lenin and the Russian Revolution, 1894–1921

Imperial Russia

The first part of the syllabus is about Imperial Russia – that means Russia as it was when ruled by the Tsars.

What you should know 👍

To be successful in this section you must be able to:

★ describe the Tsarist system of government and be able to use the word 'autocracy' and 'autocratic'

★ describe the harsh living and working conditions of Russians in both towns and the countryside

★ explain why the peasants and industrial workers were so unhappy

★ explain what Russification was.

The Tsarist state

In 1894 the huge Russian Empire was ruled by Tsar Nicholas II. Russia was an autocracy, which meant the Tsar had total power and he was against any change. The Okhrana, the Tsar's secret police, had spies everywhere and they made sure that any protest or discontent was soon dealt with. The autocracy depended on three powerful groups: the nobility, the Church and the army. They, in turn, depended on the Tsar for their power, their wealth and their privileges.

The army remained loyal to the Tsar and was used to put down any opposition to the Tsar by force. This was especially important in the lands outside Russia which had been absorbed into the Imperial state.

Within Russia the Cossacks struck terror into any groups persecuted by the Imperial state, such as Jews. Jews frequently suffered pogroms, or attacks, by the authorities.

The Church was another important method of controlling the people. Priests in every town and village taught that the Tsar was the 'Little Father' of all the Russian people, given to them by God to rule them and who must therefore be obeyed.

Russian power was also increased by the policy of Russification. That meant that in states controlled by Russia, the local culture and language was restricted and the Russian language had to be spoken.

Ordinary Russians suffered from high taxes, high rents and low wages. Discontent grew with the corrupt and inefficient way that Russia was governed and with the terrible living and working conditions faced by most Russians. However, the bulk of the people supported the Tsar and still thought of him as 'The Little Father', given to them by God to rule them.

Key words

Autocracy – a system of government in which one person has absolute power.

Emancipation – to be made free and no longer owned as a slave.

Okhrana – The secret police.

Romanovs – the family name of the Russian royal family.

Russification – making countries taken over by Russia speak only Russian in an attempt to make them lose their old national identities.

Serf – a Russian peasant worker owned by a landowner.

Tsarist state – the control of Russia by the Tsar.

At the start of the twentieth century the Russian industrial worker worked on average an eleven-hour day. Factory conditions were harsh and often unsafe and attempts to improve conditions by forming a trade union were often attacked.

In the countryside, peasants had only had their freedom since 1861 when Tsar Alexander II had emancipated the serfs. That means, for the first time, peasants working in Russian farming were not property to be bought and sold. However, land problems remained a major issue for the government.

Peasants and landowners were unhappy when the serfs were freed in 1861. Peasants still remained linked to their village commune (mir) and were not allowed to go to cities and look for work with better pay and conditions. They were also angry at the repayments (called redemption payments) they had to make for the land they were now allowed to farm on. The landowners were also unhappy. They had lost the free labour of their serfs and a large amount of land. As a result by 1905 many were facing huge debts.

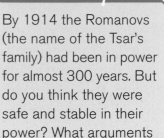

Time to reflect

By 1914 the Romanovs (the name of the Tsar's family) had been in power for almost 300 years. But do you think they were safe and stable in their power? What arguments could you use to say they were or were not?

The 1905 Revolution

The second part of the syllabus is about the 1905 Revolution – why it happened, what happened and what happened afterwards.

What you should know

To be successful in this section you must be able to:

★ describe why the 1905 Revolution broke out
★ describe what the different revolutionary groups in Russia wanted to achieve
★ explain why the revolution failed
★ explain exactly how Stolypin's policies helped to make Tsarist Russia more stable between the 1905 Revolution and the First World War.

Key words

Bolsheviks – a group of revolutionaries who wanted sudden violent change. They were not prepared to work with other political groups.
Lenin – the leader of the Bolsheviks.
Mensheviks – another group of revolutionaries who wanted slower, more peaceful change working with other political groups.
Revolution – an attempt to overthrow the government.
Soviets – local groups of workers who took over the running of their areas.

Why it happened

The revolution of 1905 was the first time the Tsar had faced open opposition from so many groups in Russian society at the same time.

A long-term cause of the 1905 Revolution was the continuing unhappiness of both peasants and landowners. Living and working conditions in Russia's industrial towns were bad. Workers worked in poorly ventilated factories for long hours and little pay. They had no trade unions for protection. Their homes were crowded and poorly built. Economic recession led to growing unemployment.

Another trigger for revolution was Russia's defeat in the Russo–Japanese War. The Tsar had hoped that a short war and an easy victory would distract the workers and provide a 'feel good factor' for the Russian people. Instead, defeat increased discontent.

What happened

A wave of strikes swept across Russia. The strikes reached their peak between December 1904 and January 1905.

The most famous strike resulted in the main trigger of revolution – Bloody Sunday. On Sunday 22 January 1905, a procession of unarmed demonstrators marched to the Winter Palace (the official residence of the Tsar in St Petersburg) to deliver a petition to the Tsar. Their demands included shorter working hours and a minimum wage. The procession was led by Father Gapon. The troops guarding the Winter Palace opened fire on the marchers causing hundreds of deaths, including women and children. The event shocked the Russian population and was swiftly followed by strikes and protests.

On 18 February, Tsar Nicholas II agreed to the creation of a new parliament called a duma. However, the duma had no power to make real change so the revolution continued.

Finally, the October Manifesto, written by Sergei Witte and issued by the Tsar, stopped the revolution by dividing the protestors. The October Manifesto gave the middle class basic political rights. The redemption payments that were hated by the peasants were ended. That left only the workers in the towns and they were dealt with by the army and the police.

The revolution fizzled out. The protestors had no real leader or main idea. Mutinies in the navy, such as onboard the Battleship *Potemkin*, were crushed. Nationalist groups, such as Poles, Finns and Lithuanians, who were angry about Russification all tried to become independent, but these groups quickly started to argue among themselves.

Opposition groups

There were some organised opposition groups to the Tsar's rule but they had little effect in the 1905 Revolution. There were three main groups.

1 **The Kadets** wanted to introduce parliamentary democracy as in the USA, France and Great Britain. This group achieved some success with the establishment of the duma in 1906. However, the duma was really just a talking-shop and had no real influence over the Tsar.

2 **The Social Revolutionaries** wished to create a new Russian society based on the old traditional style community of the peasant village. That was unlikely to happen in the industrial cities.

3 **The Social Democrats** believed in the writings of Karl Marx. Marx predicted that the industrial workers in each country would rise against the middle and upper classes and seize control. This theory is known as communism.

The Social Democrats aimed to overthrow the Tsar, the aristocracy and the Church and replace them with small councils, or **'Soviets'**, which would represent the ordinary people.

However, the Social Democrats were split among themselves. On one side were the **Bolsheviks**, led by **Lenin**. Lenin and the Bolsheviks believed that a communist revolution in Russia could only be achieved under the guidance of a small group of professional revolutionaries under his command.

The other group in the Social Democrats was the **Mensheviks**. The Mensheviks also wanted a communist revolution, but one that was democratic and not controlled by one person or a small group.

What happened afterwards

Stolypin's reforms

In 1906, unrest, discontent and violence still continued across Russia. In that year the Tsar made Pieter **Stolypin** Prime Minister. Stolypin is remembered as the man who brought stability and improvements to the Tsarist state.

Stolypin immediately organised the arrest and trial of trouble-makers; so many were hanged that the hangman's rope was called 'Stolypin's necktie'.

Stolypin did not just use violence. He also introduced land reforms in order to solve peasant complaints and he tried to improve the lives of urban workers.

Time to reflect

Why did the revolution of 1905 fail? If you were planning a future revolution, what lessons would you have learned from 1905?

Russia in the First World War

The third part of the syllabus is about Russia in the First World War.

What you should know

To be successful in this section you must be able to:

★ describe the effects of the First World War on Russia
★ explain why military defeat, economic hardship and the role of Rasputin all combined to make the Tsar very unpopular
★ describe the events of the February Revolution, 1917
★ explain fully why the First World War was the main reason for the collapse of Tsarism
★ explain why discontent with the Provisional Government grew during the summer of 1917.

Key words

Kerensky – the leader of the Provisional Government.
Provisional Government – a temporary government set up after the Tsar abdicated.
Rasputin – a mysterious monk who had a big influence over the Tsar and his wife.

The effect of the First World War on Russia

In August 1914, Russia joined the First World War.

The Russian army was badly led, while its soldiers were poorly trained and equipped. In 1915, the Tsar took personal control of the army. This was a mistake since all of Russia's problems in the war could now be directly blamed on him.

Tsar Nicholas II inspects troops during the First World War.

Confidence in the Tsar fell even further when it was discovered that a mysterious monk called Rasputin was more or less controlling the Russian government while the Tsar was away with his armies. Rasputin claimed to be able to cure the Tsar's son of a disease called haemophilia, but there were also rumours of an affair between Rasputin and the Tsar's wife, Alexandra. To make things worse, the Tsar's wife was German and some Russians thought she was a spy.

Meanwhile, in the cities, food and fuel shortages increased discontent with the Tsar. By the winter of 1916/17 the Russian army was facing defeat and in the cities, especially St Petersburg, bread and fuel queues increased and the people became angrier.

Support for the Tsar was vanishing.

Revolution part 1 – February 1917

By February 1917, the Tsarist government was in chaos. The war took fifteen million men from the farms and trains being used for the war effort were unable to be used to bring food to the cities.

In late February 1917, riots started in St Petersburg about the food shortages and the war. Finally, the Tsar abdicated and Tsarism was at an end.

Revolution part 2 – October 1917

The Provisional Government, led by Alexander Kerensky, ruled Russia from February until October 1917. It was eventually overthrown by a revolution organised by the Bolsheviks led by Lenin.

Discontent with the Provisional Government increased through 1917. The Provisional government made three big mistakes.

1 The government decided to continue with the war. Defeats continued and soldiers deserted in their tens of thousands.
2 The government allowed Lenin to return from exile. Even before Lenin returned, the government was facing problems with local councils called Soviets. These were not controlled by the Provisional

Government and contained many Bolshevik supporters. When Lenin returned to Russia he declared, 'All Power to the Soviets'. To make matters worse, Lenin promised the people **'peace, bread, land and freedom'** if they supported the Bolsheviks.

3 Throughout the summer of 1917 the Provisional Government was losing its influence. Lenin said there should be no co-operation between the Soviets and the Provisional Government. The Soviets were under Bolshevik control.

Kerensky tried to destroy Soviet power during the July Days of 1917, but he failed. When General Kornilov tried to use his army to overthrow the Provisional Government, Kerensky panicked. He gave the Bolsheviks weapons to help fight against Kornilov. When the threat from Kornilov faded the Bolsheviks simply refused to give back their weapons!

Time to reflect ❗

After the February Revolution, was the October Revolution inevitable? Did Kerensky throw away the Provisional Government's chances of success or did Lenin cause the downfall of the Provisional Government?

The October 1917 Revolution

The fourth part of the syllabus is about the October 1917 Revolution – why it happened, what happened and what happened afterwards.

What you should know

To be successful in this section you must be able to:

★ describe the events of the October Revolution
★ use accurately and appropriately, the words 'Cheka' and 'Red Terror'
★ explain why the Bolsheviks won the civil war
★ describe the effects of Bolshevik rule on Russia
★ explain what 'war communism' was
★ explain why Lenin thought war communism was necessary.

Key words

Brest-Litovsk – the name of the treaty in which Russia surrendered to Germany in 1918.

Cheka – the secret police of the Bolsheviks.

Red Army – the Bolshevik army.

Reds and Whites – the opposite sides in the civil war.

Trotsky – a Bolshevik leader and organiser of the Red Army.

War communism – Lenin's ruthless takeover of resources to feed the Red Army and force communism on the people.

The October Revolution

Between 24 and 26 October 1917, the Bolsheviks overthrew the Provisional Government.

After the October Revolution, Russia was ruled by the Bolsheviks. Lenin, leader of the Bolsheviks, believed the revolution had to be followed by a 'dictatorship of the proletariat', which really meant destroying any opposition. A new secret police, called the Cheka, was created and they began a policy called 'Red Terror' against anyone who disagreed with the Bolsheviks. By the summer of 1918, the Bolsheviks had banned all other political parties.

The Soviet state

Lenin and the Bolsheviks were determined not to share power. When elections were held for the new government, called the Constituent Assembly, the Bolsheviks only received one third of the votes. Lenin immediately ordered the Assembly to be broken up and there were no more elections. All opposition was crushed by the Cheka.

The new government established a communist state in Russia. It abolished private ownership of land and redistributed it among the peasants. Banks were nationalised and workers' control over factory production was introduced.

In March 1918, Lenin agreed to the Treaty of Brest-Litovsk which ended the war against Germany. Russia lost huge amounts of land, resources and money but did gain peace. Lenin had delivered his promise of peace, at least for a short time.

Lenin believed that the revolution would soon spread across Europe and his emergency control over Russia could then be relaxed.

The civil war

The Russian civil war broke out in 1918 and the fighting continued until 1922.

Lenin and the Bolsheviks were known as the Reds. The Whites were groups who were opposed to the Bolsheviks.

The Whites were supported by Russia's former allies Britain and France. They wanted to keep Russia in the First World War. The Red Army was led by Trotsky. He knew that two things were needed for a Bolshevik victory.

1 Firstly, the Red troops must be kept loyal, or at least be scared to run away. They knew that if they deserted they would be shot and their families severely punished.

2 Secondly, Red Army soldiers needed to be kept supplied with food, weapons and equipment. This would be more difficult.

War communism

Lenin began a new policy, called war communism, to guarantee food supplies to the cities and the Red Army. Land was taken over by the Bolsheviks. It became illegal to employ people or sell anything for a profit. Red Army squads went into the country to seize food supplies from villages.

A huge famine swept over Russia caused by war communism.

At the Kronstadt naval base, Bolshevik sailors and soldiers mutinied and said they would not accept Bolshevik orders until war communism was stopped.

Eventually, war communism stopped in March 1921, but by then the civil war had been won.

The credit for the Red Army victory should go to Trotsky, who travelled constantly from front line to front line in his armoured train. The Reds controlled the rail network and they also had a united idea of what they wanted to achieve.

In contrast, the Whites did not co-operate and they all had their own agendas. Most importantly, when the First World War ended in November 1918, the Allies saw little point in keeping up their support for the White armies, and so their strength dwindled.

Time to reflect !

Was the communist state better, worse or very similar to the Tsarist state? What are the reasons for your decision?

For practice

The following questions are examples of the types of questions you can expect within each of the three parts of the syllabus.

Imperial Russia

Describe the system of government in Russia in 1900. (4 marks)

You need to make **four** separate points from recall. You could mention that:

- the Tsar had absolute power
- the system of government depended on three groups – the nobility, the Church and the army
- these groups depended on the Tsar for their power
- there was no democracy
- ordinary people had no power or influence
- the system was described as an autocracy.

You can always gain an extra mark if you bring in more information to back up a point you are making.

For example: *Under the system of government in Russia, the Tsar had absolute power* (1 mark). *This meant that the Tsar did not have to consult anyone when he made important decisions* (1 extra mark).

Evaluate the usefulness of Source A as evidence about the way Russia was ruled by the Tsar. (5 marks)

Source A is a description of Tsar Nicholas II by Alexander Kerensky, written in his memoirs, published in 1934.

> The daily work of a monarch he found incredibly boring. He could not stand listening to or reading long reports prepared by his ministers. He liked ministers who could tell an amusing story and who did not weary his attention with too much business. When it came to defending his right to rule he became cunning, stubborn, cruel and at times merciless.

You need to make **five** clear points about the usefulness of the source.

You would probably start by arguing that the source does provide useful evidence about the way the Tsar ruled.

You should comment on who wrote the source, when it was written and why it was written. You must also state why each of the points you are writing about makes the source useful as evidence:

- the source was written by someone who had experienced the Tsar's rule
- it was written to describe the way the Tsar ruled the country.

You should also comment on what the source says:

- he tells us that the Tsar was bored by his duties as ruler
- he tells us that the Tsar didn't like long reports from his ministers
- he tells us that he could be cunning, stubborn, cruel and merciless when defending his right to rule.

You could decide however that in some ways the source is less useful because:

- it was written some time after the Tsar's death
- the author was an enemy of the Tsar who helped bring about his downfall so he could be biased.

You could also decide however that in some ways the source is less useful because of important information that has not been mentioned, such as:

- the Tsar made bad decisions e.g. leaving St Petersburg for the front in 1916
- the Tsar occasionally made concessions to reform e.g. introduction of the duma.

$\Rightarrow$

The 1905 Revolution

To what extent was defeat in the Russo–Japanese War the main cause of the 1905 Revolution? (9 marks)

Write a short introduction showing you understand there were other factors which contributed to the 1905 revolution. List these factors in your introduction.

You should then explain why the war was important. You could mention that:

- the Tsar's plan for a short successful war to boost his popularity backfired
- Russians blamed the Tsar for the humiliating defeat
- Russians were angry that many lives had been lost due to incompetent leadership.

You should then balance your answer by giving other reasons for the outbreak of the revolution, such as:

- there was growing poverty among workers and peasants
- there was rising unemployment in the cities
- there were food shortages
- the cruelty of the Tsar's government/secret police.

You should finish with a conclusion giving an overall answer to the question and support it with a reason for the judgement you have made.

For example: *Overall, the war was the most important cause of the 1905 Revolution because it provided the spark which led to the explosion of discontent against the Tsar.*

Russia in the First World War

Describe the impact of the First World War on Russia's cities. (4 marks)

You need to make **four** separate points from recall. You could mention that:

- the rail network was disrupted as military supplies took priority
- people were starving due to lack of food
- they were freezing due to lack of fuel
- there was growing anger due to defeats and casualties at the front
- rising food prices and lack of food led to bread riots
- people were protesting openly against the Tsar's rule
- protests were influenced by deserting soldiers returning to the cities.

You can always gain an extra mark if you bring in more information to back up a point you are making.

For example: *The war caused disruption to the rail network as military supplies took priority* (1 mark). *This meant that urgent supplies often failed to reach the cities* (1 extra mark).

Explain the reasons why the Rasputin affair contributed to the growing unpopularity of the Tsar. (6 marks)

You need to make **six** separate points from recall. You could mention that:

- Rasputin was believed to have a lot of influence over the Tsar's decisions
- Rasputin's influence over Russian government grew when the Tsar left St Petersburg in 1916
- ministers were fired or appointed on Rasputin's advice
- Rasputin had a bad reputation for drunkenness/womanising
- the Tsar and his wife made excuses for Rasputin's excessive behaviour
- the Rasputin affair added to growing hatred of the Tsarina (the Tsar's wife)
- Rasputin was rumoured to be part of a pro-German conspiracy.

You can always gain an extra mark if you bring in more information to back up a point you are making.

For example: *Rasputin was believed to have a lot of influence over the Tsar's decisions* (1 mark). *There were rumours the Tsar took Rasputin's advice on matters in which the monk had no expertise* (1 extra mark).

The October 1917 Revolution

Evaluate the usefulness of Source B as evidence about the failures of the Provisional Government. (5 marks)

Source B is from a speech made by Lenin in April 1917.

> Do not believe in the promises of the Provisional Government. They are deceiving you and the whole of the Russian people. The people need peace; the people need bread; the people need land. And they give you war, hunger, no bread and leave the landlords still on the land. We must fight for the social revolution.

You need to make **five** clear points about the usefulness of the source.

You would probably start by arguing that the source does provide useful evidence about the failures of the Provisional Government.

You should comment on who wrote the source, when it was written and why it was written. You must also state why the each of the points you are writing about makes the source useful as evidence. You could mention that:

- the speech was made by someone who lived in Russia under the Provisional Government
- it was made at a time when the Provisional Government was failing
- it was written to explain the failures of the Provisional Government.

You should also comment on what the source says:

- that the Provisional Government is deceiving the Russian people
- that the Provisional Government is ignoring the wishes of the people
- that a social revolution is needed.

You could decide however that in some ways the source is less useful because:

- the author (Lenin) was an enemy of the government and helped bring about its downfall so he could be biased.

You could decide however that in some ways the source is less useful because of important information that has not been mentioned, such as:

- the Provisional Government failed to hold elections
- the Provisional Government faced opposition from the powerful Petrograd Soviet.

Compare the views in Sources C and D as evidence about the reasons for the Bolshevik success in October 1917. (4 marks)

Sources C and **D** discuss the reasons for the success of the October Revolution.

Source C

> It was very clear that despite what they said the Bolsheviks did not have the support of Russian people. The October Revolution was not inevitable. The Bolsheviks simply grabbed an opportunity to seize power for themselves. This was only possible because of the chaos caused by the First World War. The revolution was a skilfully led military operation involving only a handful of people.

Source D

> In the months leading up to the Revolution, the Bolsheviks won massive support among the workers and peasants of Russia. This was because the Bolsheviks demanded Peace, Bread and Land. The October Revolution was the result of a great uprising of the downtrodden Russian people. The Bolsheviks simply guided those who had revolted because they had enough of their misery and wanted a better life.

For this type of question you must say whether you think the sources agree or not and then support your decision by making two comparisons using evidence from the source. You can make 4 simple comparisons stating what the sources agree or disagree on, or you can support your comparison with evidence from the sources – this is called a developed comparison. Two developed comparisons are worth the full 4 marks.

For this question you would probably decide that the two sources disagree. You could then support your argument with two of the following comparisons:

- Source C says that the Bolsheviks did not have the support of the Russian people but Source D says they had massive support.
- Source C says that the revolution was caused by the chaos of war but Source D says it was brought about by people who had enough of misery/wanted a better life.
- Source C says the Bolsheviks led the revolution but Source D says they simply guided it.

How fully does Source E explain the success of the Red Army in the civil war? (6 marks)

Source E Written by Trotsky explaining why the Red Army was victorious in the Civil War.

> A flabby, panicky mob could be transformed in two or three weeks into an efficient fighting force. What was needed for this? It needed a few dozen good commanders who were experienced fighters. Communists ready to make any sacrifice for the revolution were essential. Supplies such as boots for the barefooted, underwear, food, tobacco and matches attracted new recruits who were also encouraged by an energetic propaganda campaign.

It is a good idea to start off by saying that the source explains the situation fairly well. This allows you to go on to show what **is** and what **is not** in the source to support your introductory comment. The source mentions:

- the Red Army had good commanders who were experienced fighters
- it had communists ready to make any sacrifice for the revolution
- it had supplies of food and clothing
- energetic propaganda attracted and encouraged recruits.

You should then say that the source does not mention important points such as:

- harsh discipline within the Red Army
- Trotsky's skills as a commander
- the weakness of the Whites e.g. divided leadership.

The 'open door' immigration policy of the USA until 1928

The first part of the syllabus is about the 'open door' immigration policy of the USA until 1928.

What you should know

To be successful in this section you must be able to:
★ describe how the type of immigrant arriving in the USA changed around 1900
★ explain why people in the USA began to dislike and fear these new immigrants
★ explain why attitudes towards emigrants changed quickly after 1918
★ describe what was done to close the 'open door' to immigration

The status of different ethnic groups in the USA at the end of the First World War

The Melting Pot

In 1915 the US President Woodrow Wilson said 'America is like a huge melting pot. We will mix the races together to create a new person – an American'.

It was hoped that immigrants would leave their old lives behind and mix together as Americans. This was called the melting pot idea of America, where people of many backgrounds would work hard to achieve the American dream. All immigrants came to America hoping to find a better life, where they would be free and happy.

What is the American dream?

For many Americans the 'American dream' means the opportunity for anyone, regardless of their background, to become successful if they work hard. The American dream also means equality of opportunity and the chance to 'make good'. The success of Barack Obama is considered by many as a recent example of the American dream. Obama became President in 2008, but his father came from a poor village in Kenya and he was raised by his mother in Hawaii, an American state in the middle of the Pacific Ocean.

In 1919, America's population could be broadly categorised into three groups: Native Americans, the descendents of 'old' immigrants, and newer arrivals primarily from southern, central and eastern Europe, as well as Asia.

Key words

Eugenics – the 'science' that claimed to prove that one race of people was better than others.

Immigrant – a person who migrates (moves) to another country.

Immigration restriction – stopping or limiting the numbers of immigrants entering the USA.

Jim Crow – a name given to the laws intended to treat Black Americans unfairly.

Melting pot – the idea that people from many different backgrounds could combine to make a new identity for themselves as Americans.

Open door – a policy in the USA that meant people could come from anywhere to live in the country.

Segregation – keeping people of different races apart.

What happened to Native Americans?

When the original European settlers arrived in America from Europe, they did not find an empty land – it was already inhabited by millions of people who the Europeans called 'Red Indians'.

By the middle of the nineteenth century many hundreds of Native American tribes (known as nations) had been wiped out. The US government had a policy of forcing Native Americans to live on small sections of poor-quality land called reservations, where they were barred from hunting and had to rely on government-issued food rations to survive.

In 1868, the US government had declared that all persons who were born in the USA or had become American were citizens of the United States. However, the government soon ruled that Native Americans were not citizens and could not vote. By 1918, only small improvements in the lives of Native Americans had taken place and it was not until 1924 that Congress declared that all Native Americans born in the United States were citizens.

Black Americans

By 1919, very few black people living in the USA had chosen to emigrate there. Most were the descendants of Africans who were captured and taken to America as slaves over the previous 400 years. Although they were no longer enslaved, for millions of black Americans living segregated lives, this was not a free and equal land of opportunity. In the southern states of the USA black people were discriminated against by 'Jim Crow' laws and terrorised by the Ku Klux Klan. In the north, they suffered prejudice and discrimination. The experiences of black Americans are discussed in more depth later in this book.

European and Asian immigrants

America has always been a land of immigrants. Until the middle of the nineteenth century, most immigrants came from northern Europe, in particular from Britain, Ireland, Germany and Scandinavia. Those 'older' immigrants took pride in how they had defeated the Native Americans, opened up the USA and made it a strong country.

By the end of the nineteenth century, most power in the USA was in the hands of these 'older' immigrants and a new nickname – WASP – was used to describe people descended from immigrants from northern Europe. WASP stands for White Anglo Saxon Protestant. The immigrants who were descended from northern Europeans were white, they came originally from a part of northern Europe where Angles and Saxon tribes lived centuries ago and they were mostly Protestant. Wealthier WASPS liked to think of themselves as the most powerful ethnic group in America.

During the nineteenth century, many thousands of Chinese and Japanese people had also moved to America, with many helping to build the railways. However, by 1900 the United States had already started to limit Asian immigration. The Chinese Exclusion Act of 1882 was the first important law restricting immigration into the United States. By the early 1900s, the USA had also begun to exclude Japanese immigrants.

Between 1901 and 1920, the population of the United States grew to over 105 million. During this time, almost 15 million new immigrants came to America. Almost 80 per cent of this new wave of immigrants came from eastern and southern Europe.

These new immigrants faced social and economic problems, but through hard work they believed they could achieve the American dream. These new immigrants left their homes for many reasons including persecution and economic hardship. They believed that by working hard they could build new and better lives for themselves in America.

By 1918, the USA was a multi-ethnic society, where people from all sorts of different cultures lived together. However, multi-ethnic does not mean that all racial groups were treated equally or that they treated each other with respect.

Changing attitudes to immigrants in the early twentieth century

Many WASP Americans were afraid that the arrival of new immigrants from southern and eastern Europe threatened their way of life. Many of these new immigrants were Jewish or Catholic and looked very different from the more traditional immigrants from northern Europe.

In the early twentieth century, attitudes towards immigrants began to change fast.

The Ku Klux Klan was reborn in 1915. The old Klan had focused their hatred on black Americans. Now it had a new slogan – '100 per cent American' and it campaigned against the 'new' immigrants.

Around the same time, Madison Grant published a book called *The Passing of the Great Race*. Grant argued that the 'new' immigrants were inferior to the older type of immigrants. Grant was a racist who believed people from northern Europe (Nordics) were better than other races. A new science called Eugenics (pronounced 'U-jen-iks') claimed to prove that some races were inferior to others.

Many Americans feared revolution. Following the 1917 Russian Revolution, Americans feared that communism might also spread to the USA. This fear was called 'the Red Scare'. In 1919, there was a huge wave of strikes in the USA. Many Americans claimed that the strikes were caused by new immigrants.

Another fear held by many Americans was that an increase in immigrants would make jobs and houses even harder to find. After the First World War, trades union members were trying to get better working conditions. They believed anything done to improve conditions or wages was wrecked by new workers, for example from Italy or Poland, who were prepared to work longer hours for lower wages.

Immigrants were also blamed for the spread of crime. The trial of Nicola Sacco and Bartolomeo Vanzetti in 1920 for robbery and murder is a good example of how racism and dislike of immigrants became associated with fears of organised crime and political revolution to create a very intolerant attitude towards immigrants during this period.

At the same time, the Mafia and gangsters, such as Al Capone, were grabbing the headlines. After the First World War, the USA had banned the sale of alcohol so these gangsters started supplying illegal booze. Newspapers and movies were full of stories about the threat from organised crime, which really meant the Mafia. Of course, the Mafia originated in Sicily, Italy so a link was made between serious crime and immigrants.

What did the USA do to stop immigration in the 1920s?

By 1921, the US government took its first steps towards closing the 'open door' for immigrants. It introduced a quota system which limited the number of immigrants allowed to enter the country. Only three per cent of each nationality already in the United States (according to the 1910 census) would be allowed to come into America. So, for example, if in 1910 there had been 1000 people in America who had emigrated from Malta, then after 1921 only a further three per cent from Malta (30 people in total) would be allowed into the country.

The government soon realised that the new policy would not work. By using the 1910 census, it was accepting that many thousands of 'new' immigrants could still get into the USA.

New restrictions in 1924 lowered the proportion from each country to two per cent based on the sizes of national groups in the United States at the time of the 1890 census – when there were far fewer 'new' immigrants living in the USA. By changing the rules, the US government would not have to allow so many immigrants in from southern and central Europe.

By 1929, it became even harder to gain entry to the USA. Only 150,000 immigrants a year were allowed to enter the United States and 85 per cent of these had to be immigrants from northern and western Europe. When President Coolidge hoped that 'America must be kept American' he meant that the new immigration laws should limit the number of immigrants from southern and central Europe and allow more from the more traditional areas of northern and western Europe.

By 1930, immigration from southern and eastern Europe and Asia had almost completely stopped.

Time to reflect !

To what extent was a melting pot idea ever likely to be successful? Was, and is, the American dream really possible for all Americans?

African-Americans up to 1939: 'Separate but equal'

The second part of the syllabus is about African-Americans up to 1939.

What you should know

To be successful in this section you must be able to:
★ describe how Jim Crow laws made life tough for African-Americans from the late nineteenth century onwards
★ explain why the 'separate but equal' decision of the Supreme Court in 1896 was so important to the lives of African-Americans
★ describe how the activities of the Ku Klux Klan made life difficult for African-Americans.

Key words

'Separate but equal' – the name given to a decision by the Supreme Court in 1896 that accepted segregation as acceptable in the USA.

Sharecropping – a system of farming in which farmers get help with supplies and tools throughout the growing year but then have to repay their debt at harvest time by giving a share of their crop.

Segregation

Slavery had been abolished in the 1860s, but the southern states of the USA used 'Jim Crow' laws to maintain a segregated society. A segregated society means one in which people of a different colour are kept apart. Segregation did not start to break down until 1954.

Jim Crow

'Jim Crow' was a nickname for all sorts of laws that treated black Americans unfairly. These Jim Crow laws affected every part of a black American's life. For example:
● black children were forbidden to attend school with white children
● black Americans had only restricted access to public places such as parks and restaurants
● at work they had separate bathrooms and collected their pay separately from whites
● there were strict bans on whites and blacks marrying, and cemeteries even had to provide separate graveyards.

The situation was made even worse by a decision of the Supreme Court in 1896.

Separate but equal

The Supreme Court is the most important legal court in the USA. In 1896, the Supreme Court decided that segregation of black people from white people was acceptable, but was not meant to show that one race was better than another. Their ruling was called the 'separate but equal' decision. Essentially, the separate but equal decision confirmed that Jim Crow laws were legal and acceptable across the USA.

The right to vote

By 1900, few black Americans in the South were able to vote easily despite having the legal right to do so. Many southern states made up rules (called voting qualifications) that made it very difficult for black Americans to register to vote.

The Ku Klux Klan

The Ku Klux Klan was started in the late 1860s as a way of controlling newly freed slaves through fear. The Klan terrorised rural communities with night-time raids on black households. Black Americans in the southern states lived in fear of lynching. Lynching meant that a group of white people would capture and murder a black person they believed was guilty of a crime.

The Klan had friends in high places. In the 1920s, it was powerful enough to hold large marches through Washington. Few Klansmen were arrested and in some communities, local officials helped the Klan. In some state elections only candidates who were Klan-approved were allowed to stand for election. By the late 1920s, scandals involving sex and corruption had discredited the Klan but they were still (and remain even now) a symbol of white terror seeking to deny black Americans their civil rights.

Why did sharecropping trap so many African-Americans in poverty?

When slavery ended, former slaves were officially free – but free to go where and do what? All they had known was farm work. Now that slavery had been abolished, owners of plantations would have to pay wages but many couldn't afford to. Clearly, workers wanted work and plantation owners needed workers so the sharecropping system was adopted.

Sharecropping meant that former slaves would be given plots of land to work and would be given seeds and tools and machinery to farm their land... but not for free! At the end of the harvests, the workers would pay their debts by giving a share of their crop to the plantation owner who had given them the equipment. It meant that sharecroppers were always in debt so they were seldom free to leave their farms.

> ### Time to reflect !
>
> Which of all the problems facing black Americans in the 1920s and 1930s do you think created the biggest difficulties in terms of progress towards civil rights?

The civil rights campaigns of the 1950s and 1960s

The third part of the syllabus is about the civil rights campaigns of the 1950s and 1960s.

What you should know

To be successful in this section you must be able to:

★ explain why demands for civil rights grew after the end of the Second World War
★ describe the various protest methods used in the civil rights campaigns ⇨

> ### Key words
>
> **Civil disobedience –** deliberately disobeying the law in an attempt to force a change in the law.
>
> **Civil rights –** the social and political legal rights that every person in a country should have. ⇨

★ explain the importance of Martin Luther King to the civil rights movement
★ describe how both state and national governments reacted to the civil rights protests up to 1965
★ explain whether or not the civil rights campaign had a major effect on US society by 1965.

Demonstration – protests to draw attention to a problem or complaint.
Non-violent protest – protesting in as many ways as possible but without causing hurt or damage.
Voting rights – the right to register to vote easily and then cast a vote without any threats or intimidation.

The growth of the civil rights movement after 1945

Civil rights means that all people in the country should be treated equally and fairly, regardless of colour, religion or gender.

During the Second World War, black Americans started the double V campaign, which meant they wanted victory for the USA in the Second World War but also victory for civil rights in the USA. The experiences of the Second World War motivated many black Americans to campaign for change.

The Supreme Court decision of 1896 had made Jim Crow segregation legal across the USA. Now, in 1954, the Supreme Court decided that segregation in education was wrong. This opened the door to demands for further changes because if segregation was wrong in one place then it must be wrong everywhere.

The campaign for change was assisted by the spread of television because people across the USA could see for themselves the brutality of segregation. Inspirational leaders, such as Martin Luther King, were also hugely beneficial to the campaigns.

The main stages of the civil rights campaigns up to 1964

The decision of the Supreme Court sparked off a new wave of civil rights demonstrations. In 1957, at Little Rock Central High School, Arkansas, black students who tried to join the school were met by racist mobs. The President of the USA would not accept individual states in the USA ignoring the Supreme Court's decision so he ordered 1000 US soldiers to protect the black children on their way to school.

Other campaigns of the civil rights movement of the 1950s and early

Troops were ordered in to enforce desegregation at Little Rock High School in Arkansas.

99

1960s were aimed at desegregation and changing the Jim Crow laws. Examples of the campaign include:

- The bus boycott in Montgomery, Alabama. For the first time the black population showed its economic power. The bus boycott showed what could be achieved by organised, peaceful, non-violent protest.
- Student sit-in protests against segregated lunch counters spread across the South. Non-violent protest was met with violence from white racists.
- Freedom Rides were intended to test if federal decisions to desegregate facilities on interstate highways had been obeyed. Federal law stated that all seating on interstate buses and facilities on interstate highways, such as waiting rooms and wash rooms, should be desegregated. The Freedom Riders discovered that these new laws were being ignored. 'Freedom' buses were stopped and burned. Passengers were beaten, but the Freedom riders stuck to their non-violent protest beliefs.

Birmingham 1963

In Birmingham, Alabama the new governor George Wallace declared, 'Segregation now, segregation tomorrow, segregation forever.' Martin Luther King planned demonstrations to end segregation. King knew the police chief in Birmingham was an extreme racist called Eugene 'Bull' Connor. American people watched their televisions in shock and disbelief as white officers savagely attacked schoolchildren as young as eight with powerful fire hoses, dogs and even electric cattle prods.

The events in Birmingham caused an outcry across America. President Kennedy was forced to order an end to all segregation.

Martin Luther King and 'I have a dream'

Martin Luther King believed in non-violent, peaceful protest against segregation and discrimination. He also believed that non-violent civil disobedience was the way to gain civil rights.

In August 1963, the March on Washington was arranged to increase publicity for the civil rights campaign. It worked! Hundreds of thousands of people attended the march. The inspirational speech that Martin Luther King gave to a worldwide TV audience is often called the 'I Have a Dream' speech.

The 1964 Civil Rights Act was the most important new civil rights law up to that time and it did a great deal to get rid of discrimination and segregation. It ended racial segregation in schools, the workplace and in facilities that served the general public, such as transport and lunch counters.

The right to vote

The last big civil rights issue in the South was the right to vote freely. After the passing of the Civil Rights Act in 1964, civil rights groups knew that they had to push for a voting rights law. They planned a march across Alabama and expected a strong reaction from the local police. They knew that TV news showing the police attacking peaceful demonstrators always gained support and sympathy for the civil rights campaign. What the marchers did not expect was the local police firing tear gas and then mounted police charging the marchers.

Time to reflect !

Imagine you were a black American in 1964. Would your views about the Civil Rights Act differ depending on where in the USA you lived? Would you have felt the civil rights movement had been a success?

In August 1965, Congress (part of the US government) passed the Voting Rights Act, which removed various barriers that prevented people from registering to vote.

The Voting Rights Act marked the end of the civil rights campaigns in the South.

Changes in the civil rights movement during the 1960s

The fourth part of the syllabus is about how the location and the methods of the civil rights movement changed during the 1960s.

What you should know

To be successful in this section you must be able to:

★ describe a ghetto
★ describe what black radicalism means
★ explain the importance of Stokely Carmichael and Malcolm X
★ explain how American society was affected by the civil rights campaigns up to 1968.

Key words

Black radicalism – Black groups who wanted to take direct action themselves and not 'ask' for help from white authority. Black radicals did not want to integrate.

Ghetto – a slum area of a city.

Militant – someone who is prepared to use force to get what is wanted.

Militant civil rights protests

By the early 1960s, some civil rights campaigners disagreed with Martin Luther King about the use of peaceful, non-violent protest. The most famous of these more militant leaders were Malcolm X and Stokely Carmichael.

By the late 1960s, urban race riots and new organisations such as the Black Panthers and the Nation of Islam had grabbed the headlines. These new groups, who used violent direct action in their protests, were collectively called Black Radicals. The Black Radical groups wanted improvements in housing, education and employment opportunities. They also argued that black Americans should be prepared to defend themselves and fight back, using violence if necessary. Non-violent protest was rejected as a failure.

Black Americans in the north

By 1965, half of all black Americans lived in the cities of the north and most of them lived in slum areas which were known as ghettos. As far as black Americans in the ghettos were concerned, the campaigns against segregation in the southern states of the USA were completely irrelevant to them. The problems in the ghettos were unemployment, poverty and white police bullying black Americans. New laws that ended segregation and made voting easier for black Americans did little to help the problems of black Americans in the main cities of the north.

Some historians argue that Martin Luther King's message of non-violence was old-fashioned and that 'Black Power' promised faster results.

Black Power

The main ideas of Black Power were:

- black Americans should not rely on white people to 'give' them civil rights
- white support for the civil rights movement was not wanted
- black Americans should build up their own schools, communities, businesses, even hospitals, without interference from whites.

Who was Malcolm X?

Malcolm X did not support integration (the mixing of races – the opposite of segregation) and argued that black Americans should develop their society to be separate from whites. Unlike King, who believed in the American dream, Malcolm X saw an 'American nightmare'.

Malcolm X was one of the first black activists to draw attention to the increasing urban problems within the ghettos of American cities – crime, prostitution, drugs and unemployment. His message of self-help attracted many listeners tired of having to wait for the whites in authority to improve conditions. He warned that if nothing was done, violence would erupt.

Why did riots break out in so many cities during the 1960s?

By 1965, half of all black Americans lived in the cities of the north and west. Most of them lived in ghettos. They had to put up with bad housing, high rents, unemployment, poverty and hunger. Urban gang violence and drug-related crime were also increasing.

In 1965, the Watts district of Los Angeles exploded in a riot. To restore order, 14,000 troops were required, but not one of the causes of the riot was dealt with.

The importance of the Watts Riot, and others which followed, was to show that economic and social issues were far more important to black people in the northern cities than the 'older' civil rights issues of desegregation and voting rights in the South.

How successful were the civil rights campaigns by 1968?

In 1968, King was assassinated. The year before King's death, one of the most destructive riots had taken place in Detroit. Several people were killed and millions of dollars worth of property was destroyed.

After the Detroit riot, President Johnson asked Otto Kerner to lead a commission to thoroughly investigate the causes of the urban riots. When the Kerner Commission made its report public in 1968, Americans were shocked by what it said.

The Kerner Commission concluded that:
'Our nation is moving towards two societies, one black, one white – separate and unequal'.

It went on to say that:

'What white Americans have never understood – but what the Negro can never forget – is that white society is deeply implicated in the ghetto. White institutions created it, white institutions maintain it, and white society condones it.'

In other words, the problems of the urban ghettos were not caused by 'troublemakers'. The problems of the ghettos were caused by genuine poverty that was the result of the lack of opportunities for black Americans to improve their lives. Laws had been passed to give black Americans civil rights that ended segregation and discrimination, but these laws did little to change attitudes or the reality of poverty.

Time to reflect

All the demonstrations in the South in the 1950s and early 60s were really aimed at one thing – getting rid of segregation. But if segregation was not the main problem facing African-Americans in the northern states of the USA, how relevant were the campaigns of King in the north?

For practice

The following questions are examples of the types of questions you can expect within each of the three parts of the syllabus.

The 'open door' immigration policy of the USA until 1928

Describe the impact of America's 'open door' immigration policy. (4 marks)

You need to make **four** separate points from recall. You could mention that:

- it meant that few restrictions were placed on immigration from Europe
- increasing numbers of immigrants arrived from Europe
- many immigrants arrived from Italy and eastern Europe
- immigrants supplied the labour needed for America's growing industries
- some Americans blamed new immigrants for their problems
- there was demand for restrictions on immigration by the 1920s
- the immigration was supported by those who believed America should be a 'melting pot'.

You can always gain an extra mark if you bring in more information to back up a point you are making.

For example: *The 'open door' policy meant that there were few restrictions on immigration from Europe* (1 mark). *All that an immigrant required was the cost of a ticket on a steamship* (1 extra mark).

Evaluate the usefulness of Source A as evidence about the impact of immigration to the USA before 1928. (5 marks)

Source A was written in 1918 by a person whose family had settled in America 50 years before.

> The USA should no longer be open to just any foreigner. These new immigrants cannot read or write and many have no money. We true Americans want to look after ourselves first of all. We don't want our jobs and homes taken away from us by immigrants. There are far too many people coming from southern Europe and many are Catholic or Jewish. They are not good Protestants like us.

You need to make **five** clear points about the usefulness of the source.

You would probably start by arguing that the source does provide useful evidence about the impact of immigration before 1928.

You should comment on who wrote the source, when it was written and why it was written. You must also state why each of the points you are writing about makes the source useful as evidence:

- the source was written in 1918 at a time when immigration to America was increasing
- it was written to explain why the author supports immigration restriction.

You should also comment on what the source says:

- they claim that immigrants cannot read or write
- they claim that immigrants are poor
- they claim that immigrants will take away jobs and homes from other Americans
- they claim that old immigrants should be looked after first.

You could decide however that in some ways the source is less useful because:

- it was written by an American who was not a new immigrant and therefore possibly biased.

You could also decide, however, that the source is also less useful because of important information that has not been mentioned, such as:

- that 'WASPs' had developed a strong resentment of new immigrants
- it fails to mention that literacy tests had already been imposed
- that immigrants often took jobs which others did not want
- that economic problems after 1918 contributed to racist attitudes.

African-Americans up to 1939: 'Separate but equal'

To what extent was the Ku Klux Klan the main reason why life was hard for black Americans in the 1920s and 1930s? (9 marks)

Write a short introduction showing you understand there were other factors which made life hard for black Americans in the 1920s. List these factors in your introduction.

You should then explain why the KKK was important. For example:

- the KKK prevented black Americans from obtaining justice if they were accused of a crime
- KKK intimidation and threats stopped many black Americans from standing up for themselves
- the KKK was very powerful because it had supporters inside the police and government.

You should then balance your answer by giving other reasons why life was hard for black Americans in the 1920s:

- the Jim Crow laws meant that black Americans had a poorer standard of education
- these laws also prevented black Americans from using the same shops, restaurants and cinemas as whites
- it was made very difficult for black Americans to register to vote.

You should finish with a conclusion that gives an overall answer to the question and support it with a reason for the judgement you have made.

For example:

The KKK was an important reason why life was hard for black Americans, but the real problem was that nothing would change unless black Americans could use the vote.

Evaluate the usefulness of Source B as evidence of the reasons for the popularity of the Ku Klux Klan in the 1920s. (5 marks)

Source B was written in 1972 by an American man brought up in the South in the 1920s.

It may be asked why the town took so enthusiastically to the Klan? Older, more traditional Americans believed they were in danger of being overrun. The 'foreigners were ruining our country' and so anything 'foreign' was 'un-American' and a menace. Cars were draped with the American flag and some were painted with Klan slogans with homemade signs such as 'America for the Americans.'

You need to make **five** clear points about the usefulness of the source.

You would probably start by arguing that the source does provide useful evidence about why the Ku Klux Klan was popular in the 1920s.

You should comment on who wrote the source, when it was written and why it was written. You could mention that:

- the source was written by a person who was brought up in the South where the Klan was active
- it was written to explain why his town supported the Klan.

You should also comment on what the source says:

- he says that some Americans felt that the country was being overrun by foreigners
- he says that some feared that America was being ruined by foreigners
- he says that the Klan appealed to patriotism. For example, cars were draped in the American flag/there were 'America for the Americans' slogans.

However, you could decide that in some ways the source is less useful because:

- it was written many years after the event so may not be accurate.

You could also decide, however, that the source is less useful because of important information that has not been mentioned, such as that:

- the Klan was also popular among those who still resented the rights given to black Americans
- the Klan had infiltrated many positions of authority, for example, in business, politics and the police
- the Klan made effective use of intimidation and propaganda.

The civil rights campaigns of the 1950s and 1960s

Explain the reasons for the growth of the civil rights movement in the 1950s and the 1960s. (6 marks)

You need to make **six** separate points from recall. You could mention:

- the hardship and humiliation caused by the Jim Crow laws
- the segregation of schools, transport, etc.
- the inequality faced by black Americans in employment and housing
- the impact of the Second World War (for example, black servicemen overseas now had some experience of integration)
- refusal of southern states to desegregate following the 'Brown v Board of Education' ruling of 1954
- the success of the Montgomery bus boycott
- the effective leadership of the movement, e.g. Martin Luther King
- the success of protests, for example, in Birmingham, Washington and Selma
- the growing support from white Americans, for example through student groups like CORE.

You can always gain an extra mark if you bring in more information to back up a point you are making. For example: *The hardship and humiliation caused by Jim Crow encouraged the growth of the civil rights movement* (1 mark). *Some of these laws dated back 90 years* (1 extra mark).

Compare the views of Sources C and D as evidence of the impact of the Birmingham protests. (4 marks)

Sources C and **D** describe the impact of the Birmingham protests.

Source C

> A week after the attack by Bull Connor's police, the civil rights movement seemed to have won a great victory. The world had been shocked by pictures of young children being attacked by police dogs and washed down streets by fire hoses. The black residents of Birmingham benefited when President Kennedy ordered an end to segregation in Birmingham and better treatment of its black residents. The protests boosted the reputation of Martin Luther King.

Source D

> Martin Luther King lost the support of many black civil rights activists as a result of his tactics at Birmingham. This was a victory which came at great cost; many protesters had suffered serious injury and three students from the north were murdered shortly afterwards. Even some of King's supporters wondered if his tactics were justified. Once the TV cameras left Birmingham, black residents experienced a serious backlash of white hostility.

For this type of question you must say whether you think the sources agree or not and then support your decision by making two comparisons using evidence from the source. You can make 4 simple comparisons stating what the sources agree or disagree on, or you can support your comparison with evidence from the sources – this is called a developed comparison. Two developed comparisons are worth the full 4 marks.

For this question you would probably decide that the two sources disagree. You could then back this up with two of the following comparisons:

- Source C says that the movement had won a great victory, but Source D says it was achieved at great cost.
- Source C says that black residents of Birmingham benefited from the protest, but Source D says that they faced a backlash after the TV cameras had gone.
- Source C says that the march boosted King's reputation, but source D says he lost the support of many activists.

Changes in the civil rights movement in the 1960s

How fully does Source E explain the ideas of Malcolm X? (6 marks)

Source E describes the ideas of Malcolm X.

> Malcolm X said that non-violent tactics should be abandoned because they had led to black protesters being beaten and even killed. Other radical leaders were now demanding respect and equality for black people. Malcolm saw black people in America as a different race with their own ideas and culture. He wanted black people to have separate communities of their own rather than following Martin Luther King's dream of black Americans becoming integrated into white society.

It is a good idea to start by saying that the source explains the ideas of Malcolm X fairly well. This allows you to go on to show what *is* and what *is not* in the source to support your introductory comment.

The source mentions:

- that non-violence led to many black people being beaten and killed
- that Malcolm X saw black Americans as a different race
- Malcolm X wanted black Americans to have separate communities.

You should then say that the source does not mention important points such as:

- Malcolm X converted to Islam and adopted its beliefs
- he shared the aims of the Nation of Islam
- he wanted more rights for black people in the northern cities
- his ideas changed in later life. For example, he became more willing to co-operate with white people.

Part Three: Model answers to exam-style questions

This section will provide you with full examples of answers written by candidates for all the different types of questions. The questions are from all the different sections and parts covered in this book. After each answer, an examiner has written comments on why the answers are either weak or good. If you study what has been done well and what has been done poorly you will get an idea of how you should write your own answers.

Chapter 11
Migration and Empire, 1830–1939

Example

Question

Explain why many Irish came to Scotland in the nineteenth century. (6 marks)

Answer 1

Many Irish come to Scotland in the nineteenth century because many had died in the potato famine. All the potatoes were turned into foul smelling grey mush. Some families had to eat grass. They had nothing else to eat. The famine caused the deaths of millions of people across Ireland. People left their country never to return.

Why is this a weak answer?

The answer only deals with the potato famine and doesn't actually explain why this led people to leave Ireland (push factors) nor why they chose to come to Scotland (pull factors).

   Marks given 0/6

Answer 2

There were several reasons why Irish people came to Scotland in the nineteenth century. Better wages were a big attraction and so was regular employment because Irish immigrants had been farm workers who had faced low wages and times of no work at all. In Scotland, work was also available for the whole family in the factories of central Scotland. That would mean the family could earn more than they had done in Ireland. There were also push factors that forced people to emigrate. The potato famine gave people a choice of starve or emigrate. Even before the famine, poverty was a huge problem in Ireland and the prospect of better jobs caused many Irish to think of emigration as an answer to their problems and an opportunity for a better life.

Why is this a good answer?

The answer contains at least six reasons and each of these points is explained or developed in a way that helps answer the question.

   Marks given 6/6

Example

Question

How fully does **Source A** describe Scottish attitudes towards Irish immigrants?

Source A is about attitudes to Irish immigrants.

> The Irish are dirty and bring disease wherever they settle. It is no coincidence that the cholera plagues us whenever the Irish live nearby. Our honest Scotsmen struggle to find work while the Irish who steal our jobs are only too happy to make us paupers by forcing our wages down. They hide themselves away in slums in our cities and refuse to mix with the good Scots folk. Their priests keep them tied to their superstitions. Get rid of them!

Answer 1

The source partly describes Scottish attitudes towards Irish immigrants.

It points out that the Irish were blamed for spreading diseases like cholera. It shows that Scots believed that the Irish were stealing jobs from them and that Irish immigrants were criticised for not mixing with the Scots.

Why is this a weak answer?

The answer includes three points from the source but there is no recall. Answers which refer only to the source are likely to gain no more than 2 marks.

  Marks given 2/6

Answer 2

The source partly describes Scottish attitudes towards Irish immigrants.

It points out that the Irish were blamed for spreading diseases like cholera. It shows that Scots believed that the Irish were stealing jobs from them and that Irish immigrants were criticised for not mixing with the Scots.

However, the source doesn't mention that Irish immigrants were also accused of drunkenness and that they had an unfair reputation for breaking strikes. The source does not mention that some Scots and Irish worked together in trade unions and the temperance movement.

Why is this a good answer?

This answer makes three clear points from the source and then adds three further reasons from recall.

  Marks given 6/6

Example

Question

Evaluate the usefulness of Source A as evidence about the problems facing women in the early 1900s. (5 marks)

Source A

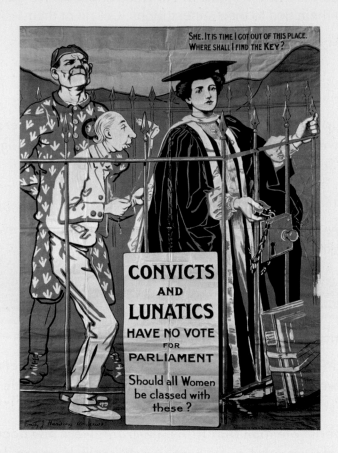

Answer 1

This source is useful as it is a primary source which was produced at the time. It was produced by the Suffragettes and shows that women are being treated the same as convicts and lunatics when it comes to getting the vote. The source does not show other things that women did to win the vote such as setting fire to racecourses.

Why is this a weak answer?

The answer attempts a balanced evaluation of the source but is too short and lacks detail. Just saying it is a primary source is not enough to gain a mark unless a point is made about when the source was produced. Simply pointing out that the source was produced by the Suffragettes is not enough without saying something about who the Suffragettes were.

The point about what the source does not show is not relevant to the question.

Marks given 0/5

⇨

Answer 2

The poster is partly useful as evidence of problems faced by women in the early 1900s. It was produced in the early 1900s when women faced many inequalities, making it useful because it is primary evidence written at the time. It is useful because it was published by the Suffragettes to show that women were being treated unequally when it came to the vote. It is useful because it describes accurately that women are treated no better than convicts and lunatics when it comes to having the right to vote in parliamentary elections. It is useful because it shows accurately that women are finding it difficult to improve their rights — 'where shall I find the key'?

On the other hand the poster, produced by the WSPU, does contain some bias showing an educated woman in contrast to convicts and lunatics. The poster is less useful because it does not show many of the problems of working-class women such as low wages and domestic abuse.

Why is this a good answer?

The answer is balanced by looking at the usefulness and also the limitations of the source.

Positive evaluation points about the source are made by commenting on when (one mark) and why (one mark) the source was produced. Two important, relevant points about the problems facing women are taken from the source (one + one marks). Evidence showing the bias of the source is included (one mark) and the answer is finished with a list of some of the problems which are not mentioned in the source (one mark).

Marks given 5/5

Example

Question

To what extent was low pay the main reason for the unrest on Red Clydeside in 1919? (9 marks)

Answer 1

Low pay led to strikes and protests on Clydeside in 1919. Working people also wanted a 40-hour working week. A great crowd gathered together in Glasgow's George Square. The government over-reacted and sent soldiers and tanks on to the streets which led to fighting. The red flag was raised which showed that protesters had heard about the workers' revolution in Russia. Tension had been building up in Glasgow for years. During the war, for example, there had been rent strikes.

Overall, there were many reasons for the unrest on Red Clydeside in 1919 including low pay, government over-reaction and the revolution in Russia.

Why is this a weak answer?

The answer loses 4 marks because it is not structured properly. There is no clear introduction and no proper conclusion: the last sentence is just a summary of some of the points made with no attempt to judge their importance. There are five relevant points but there is no attempt to organise them into a balanced answer which means that a maximum of 3 marks can be awarded.

Marks given 3/9

Answer 2

Low pay contributed to unrest on Red Clydeside in 1919 but there were other factors such as long hours, news of the Russian Revolution and government provocation.

Workers on the Clyde had seen their wages fall during the war. At the beginning of 1919 there was a campaign to raise wages to £1 per day. This led to the calling of a strike in January which was supported by most workers in Glasgow.

However, there were other reasons for unrest. Workers also protested for a shorter working week. News of the revolution in Russia had encouraged workers to stand up for their rights. In January 1919 the government increased the unrest by sending troops and tanks on to the streets of Glasgow which led to fighting between workers and soldiers.

Overall, low pay was one of the reasons for the unrest on Red Clydeside but the unrest was so great that there must have been more to it.

Why is this a good answer?

The answer is worth full marks because it has a clear introduction and contains at least five clear points which are carefully organised into a balanced answer. The conclusion makes a judgement which is supported with a reason.

Marks given 9/9

Chapter 13

The Atlantic Slave Trade, 1770–1807

Example

Question

Describe the experience of the middle passage for male slaves. (4 marks)

Answer 1

Slaves on the middle passage had a terrible time. They were chained below decks where they were forced to lay on their backs. They suffered from terrible diseases and were beaten up a lot. There was never enough food or water. One time, the first mate took a female slave to the captain's cabin to spend the night. She was called a 'belly warmer'.

Why is this a weak answer?

The answer starts okay and would get a mark for commenting on how the slaves were kept. But then the answer becomes too vague. The candidate should have attempted to say a bit more about diseases, such as smallpox. Slaves did not always go hungry on the middle passage – the crew would try to make sure the slaves were fed because they would earn more money if the slaves were healthy when they were sold. The last point would get no marks. Try to avoid describing single incidents like this which might have happened – stick to the facts about what happened.

Marks given 1/4

Answer 2

Male slaves spent most of the time below deck in the dark hold of the ship. They were packed closely together which was very unhealthy because disease could spread. They were fed regularly, usually on horse-beans and yams. If they refused to eat they would have their mouths forced open by the crew. The male slaves were given regular exercise to keep them as fit and strong as possible. Sometimes, the male slaves would try to overwhelm the crew and take over the ship.

Why is this a good answer?

The answer makes at least four clear, relevant points from recall. Each of these points is explained or developed in a way that helps answer the question. The answer includes a developed point about food on the middle passage. The kinds of foods given to slaves are described and then the candidate makes an additional point about the forced feeding of slaves.

Marks given 4/4

Example

Question

Evaluate the usefulness of Source A as evidence of the importance of the slave trade to Britain. (5 marks)

Source A was written by a slave trader in 1790.

> It would be impossible to continue the success of the West Indies and to keep up the present rate of sugar production without the continuing trade in slaves. Unless we continue to import slaves, the numbers working on the plantations will go down and the crops will decline. Then the population of these islands, just like the crops, will be extinct in no time.

Answer 1

Source A is very useful because it says that they couldn't keep up the rate of sugar production without trade in slaves. If slaves were not imported the population of these islands would fall and would be extinct like the crops.

Why is this a weak answer?

Although it is not a straight copy, the answer has done very little with the source. It might gain one mark for relevant information, but there is no real attempt to weigh up the usefulness of the authorship, timing or purpose of the source.

Marks given 1/5

Answer 2

Source A is partly useful as evidence about the importance of the slave trade. It is useful because it was written when Britain's trade in slaves was at its height. It was written by someone involved in the trade so he would know a lot about it. The source is useful because it was written to explain why the trade was so important to Britain. It points out accurately that sugar could not be grown in the same quantities without the use of slaves.

However, it is less useful because the author is a trader who is likely to be making a lot of money out of the trade and is therefore biased and may be exaggerating its importance to Britain. This might make the source less reliable as evidence about the importance of the slave trade to Britain.

Why is this a good answer?

The answer is balanced by looking at the usefulness and also the limitations of the source.

Positive evaluation points about the source are made by commenting on the author (one mark) and when (one mark) and why (one mark) the source was produced. One relevant point is made about the importance of slaves in sugar production (one mark).

However, evidence showing the bias of the author is also included (one mark).

Marks given 5/5

Chapter 14

Changing Britain, 1760–1914

Example

Question

Describe the impact of new technology on the textile industry by the beginning of the nineteenth century. (4 marks)

Answer 1

There were many important improvements in technology in the textile industry by 1800. Richard Arkwright invented the water frame in 1762. Hargreaves' Spinning Jenny was invented in 1765. Crompton's mule was first used in 1775 and Edmund Cartwright built the first steam powered loom in 1784. These inventions all helped the textile industry.

Why is this a weak answer?

The answer contains relevant and detailed information about new technology, but there is no attempt to describe its impact. Therefore, the answer would receive no marks because it does not deal with the question.

   Mark given 0/4

Answer 2

In 1765 Hargreaves' new spinning machine allowed one worker to spin many cotton threads at the same time. Richard Arkwright then invented the first water powered spinning machine which was more efficient. These new machines meant that the spinning of cotton yarn moved from workshops into factories. Crompton's mule could produce a much finer thread than Arkwright's machine. Edmund Cartwright built the first steam powered loom in 1784 which meant weaving also moved into factories.

Why is this a good answer?

The answer makes at least four clear, relevant points from recall. Each of these points is explained or developed in a way that helps answer the question.

   Marks given 4/4

Example

Question

Evaluate the usefulness of Source B as evidence about the impact of the growth of the railway network. (5 marks)

Source B was written by Eric Hobsbawm, a leading British historian, in 1968.

> Between 1820 and 1850 some six thousand miles of railways were opened in Britain. In every respect this was a revolutionary transformation – more revolutionary, in its way, than the rise of the cotton industry because it affected the life of the ordinary citizen. It reached into some of the remotest areas of the countryside and the centres of the greatest cities. It transformed the speed of transport from one measured in single miles an hour to one measured in many miles per hour.

Answer 1

The source is useful as evidence of the impact of the growth of the railway network because it tells us that a lot of track was laid – 6000 miles. It is useful because it also points out that the railways reached people all over Britain and that it meant that the transport of goods and people became much quicker.

Why is this a weak answer?

The answer makes three good points about the usefulness of the content of the source as evidence of the impact of the railways. However, a maximum of two marks can be given for accurate comments on the content of a source. The answer does not comment on the origin, purpose or limitations of the source.

Marks given 2/5

Answer 2

Source B is a useful source because it was written by a leading historian who would have studied the impact of railways. It is useful because the purpose of the source is to explain the impact that railways had on Britain. It is useful because the author points out accurately the important effects of the railway such as the way it linked the countryside with the city, and also that railways transformed the speed of transport in Britain.

However, it is less useful because the author did not witness the changes and the source does not mention the damage done by the expansion of railway building in towns and the countryside.

Why is this a good answer?

The answer is balanced because it looks at the usefulness and also the limitations of the source.

Positive evaluation points about the source are made by commenting on the author (one mark) and on why (one mark) the source was produced. Two relevant points are made about the impact of railways – both their speed (one mark) and the way they linked town and countryside (one mark). However, the student wisely points out the fact that the author did not witness the impact (one mark) and the omission of some points (one mark) could make the source less useful.

Marks given 5/5

Chapter 15

The Making of Modern Britain, 1880–1951

Example

Question

How fully does **Source A** explain the reasons why the Liberals passed social reforms between 1906 and 1910.

Source A is about the reasons for the Liberal reforms between 1906 and 1910.

> The reasons for the social reforms can be explained by jealousy and fear! Our politicians cannot accept that Germany has a system to help its poor far in advance of our own. Our country has been humiliated by its poor show in the war against the Boers. Our volunteer army was shown to be reliant on the poor, weak and ill fed from our slums. Now the Liberals are in power, they are worried by the growing Labour Party who will surely gain support from the poor who, so far, have received so little help from the government. The days of Laissez Faire are dead. We must take more action to help the poor!

Answer 1

The source partly explains why the Liberals passed social reforms between 1906 and 1910. It points out that the government needed to match Germany's system for helping the poor and that the Liberals were worried that Labour would take the votes of the poor if the government didn't help them. But the source fails to mention that the Boer War had shown up the poverty that existed in the slums.

Why is this a weak answer?

The answer includes two relevant points from the source but instead of making a point from recall to balance the answer, another point from the source is added.

Marks given 2/6

Answer 2

The source partly explains why the Liberals passed social reforms between 1906 and 1910. It points out that the government felt the need to match Germany's system for helping the poor. It points out that army recruitment during the Boer war showed the poor health of people living in the slums. Also, it shows that the Liberals were worried that Labour would take the votes of the poor if the government didn't help them.

However, the source doesn't mention that the surveys of Booth and Rowntree showed the true extent of poverty and persuaded some liberal politicians that the government needed to step in to help. Also school inspectors claimed that many children were not benefitting from education because they were malnourished.

Why is this a good answer?

This answer makes three clear points from the source and then adds three further reasons from recall.

Marks given 6/6

Example

Question

Compare the views in Sources B and C about the causes of poverty in the early twentieth century. (4 marks)

Sources B and **C** are about the causes of poverty in the early twentieth century.

Source B

The investigations of Booth and Rowntree both revealed the problems facing the poorer classes in Britain. They identified some of the direct causes of poverty. The main reasons were that a man's earnings were not enough to support himself and his family. They also found it difficult to obtain employment when trade was bad. Families also faced hardship when the main wage earner was off work due to sickness.

Source C

Although many people thought Britain was experiencing a golden age, the working classes did not gain a fair share of the rewards. There was increasing unemployment and thirty per cent of the population were living in poverty due to low wages. Of those living in poverty, about two-thirds were in that position because of low pay or irregular earnings. About one quarter were poor because of illness.

Answer 1

The sources agree because Source B points out that men's earnings were not enough to support a family and that it was hard for people to find regular work.

Source C agrees by pointing out that thirty per cent of the population were poor due to low wages and that there was increasing unemployment.

Why is this a weak answer?

This answer picks out relevant points from the sources to support the judgement that the sources agree. However, it does not compare what the sources say point-by-point so would only receive two marks.

Marks given 2/4

Answer 2

The sources agree about the causes of poverty. Source B reveals that the man's earnings were not enough to support a family. Source C supports this by saying that thirty per cent of the population were in poverty due to low wages. Source B also says that it was often difficult to get employment when times were bad. Source C agrees saying that there was increasing unemployment.

Why is this a good answer?

The answer starts by pointing out that the two sources agree. It then makes two clear points of comparison. Both the comparisons are backed up with evidence from each source.

Marks given 4/4

Chapter 16

Hitler and Nazi Germany, 1919–1939

Example

Question

How successful were Nazi economic policies in reducing unemployment? (9 marks)

Answer 1

Hitler's war economy created many jobs in the armed forces and building tanks, ships and aircraft. Hitler also invested in big public works projects like the building of the autobahns. A lot of money was spent on big prestige projects, like fancy new government buildings which created thousands of jobs but they were mostly short-term. Hitler was preparing Germany for war. This created jobs in the armed forces.

Overall Hitler's economic policies reduced unemployment because his schemes like public works created a lot of jobs.

Why is this a weak answer?

The answer makes five relevant points but no attempt has been made to organise them into a proper answer. The reader is left to decide which factors are important. The last sentence gives an answer to the question but is not balanced and contradicts some of the points made in the rest of the answer.

Marks given 2/9

Answer 2

Nazi economic policies contributed to the fall in unemployment but there were other factors such as improvements in the world economy, the invasion of other countries and not counting some people as unemployed.

Nazi economic policies appeared to be very successful in reducing unemployment in Germany. After 1933 Germany saw a bigger fall in unemployment than any other country in Europe. By 1939 Hitler claimed that as a result of his economic policies Germany had zero unemployment. Everyone had a job.

However, the general improvement in the world economy in the 1930s helped reduce unemployment in Germany and this was nothing to do with Hitler's economic policy. Hitler's invasion of Austria and Czechoslovakia allowed him to plunder resources and raw materials which helped industry to grow in Germany and take on more workers. Also, Hitler forced women, Jews and Nazi undesirables out of work but did not count them as unemployed so the supposed reduction was more to do with Nazi propaganda.

Overall, Nazi economic policies didn't have much effect on unemployment but the truth was hidden by Nazi lies and propaganda.

Why is this a good answer?

The answer has a clear introduction and contains at least five clear points which are carefully organised into 'points for' and 'points against' the benefits of Hitler's economic policies. The answer finishes with a conclusion which gives a balanced answer to the question.

Marks given 9/9

Example

Question

How fully does Source A explain the reasons for the weakness of the government in Germany during the Weimar Republic? (6 Marks)

Source A explains the weakness of governments during the Weimar Republic.

> For many years the largest party, SPD refused to join any coalition. This meant that all governments had the support of less than half the members of the Reichstag, which made it difficult to rule the country. The result was that coalitions kept being defeated and new governments had to be formed. There were six different coalition governments which tried to run Germany between 1923 and 1928. The longest lasted just 21 months.

Answer 1

The source partly explains the reasons for the weakness of the government. It points out that the largest party during the Weimar Republic, the SPD, refused to join any coalition government. The SPD decided not to share power with the other parties which had done well in the election. This meant that the coalitions kept being defeated and new governments were constantly being formed. What happened was that whenever a government collapsed a new one had to be formed. The source points out that there were six different coalitions with the longest lasting 21 months.

Why is this a weak answer?

The answer includes three points from the source. However, an answer which only refers to the source can gain a maximum of 2 marks.

    Marks given 2/6

Answer 2

The source partly explains the reasons for the weakness of the government. It points out that the largest party during the Weimar Republic, the SPD, refused to join any coalition government. This meant that the coalitions kept being defeated and new governments were constantly being formed. The source points out that there were six different coalitions with the longest lasting 21 months.

    However, the source doesn't mention other factors which weakened government. Some Germans still blamed the leaders of the Republic for Germany's surrender at the end of the First World War. The Weimar Republic was always associated with acceptance of the hated Treaty of Versailles. So some nationalists opposed any Weimar government. Also Germany faced severe economic problems during the period and many Germans blamed the government for not dealing with them.

Why is this a good answer?

This answer takes three clear and relevant causes of government weakness from the source and then adds three further reasons from recall.

    Marks given 6/6

Chapter 17

Red Flag: Lenin and the Russian Revolution, 1894–1921

Example

Question

To what extent were military defeats to blame for the outbreak of the February Revolution? (9 marks)

Answer 1

The military defeats suffered by the Russian army contributed to the outbreak of revolution in Russia in February 1917 but there were other factors such as shortages of food in the cities, suffering of the peasants and hatred for the Tsarina.

By February 1917, the Russian army had faced a series of bad defeats in their battles against the German army, which was much better equipped than the Russians were. This had damaged the morale of Russian soldiers who were sick of losing battles and seeing so many of their comrades killed. They decided to mutiny and revolt against their leaders who had made so many terrible blunders. The Tsar had decided to leave his wife and family in Petrograd and take personal control of the army at the front. This meant that when things continued to go badly for the Russian army he was blamed for the defeats and this added to the reasons why the Russians wanted to get rid of him.

However, military defeats were not completely to blame for the outbreak of the February Revolution.

There were other important reasons why the people revolted against the Tsar. People in the cities faced severe shortages of food because so many of the peasants who produced the food had gone to fight. The railway system was in chaos so fuel and other supplies were not reaching the cities. Lack of fuel was a particular problem if it was a cold winter. There were also massive shortages in the countryside and peasants had had enough. Also, few Russians had any respect for the Tsarina who had been left to rule Russia. She had fallen under the influence of the 'mad monk' Rasputin who seemed to have the ability to heal her son who suffered from a rare blood disease. Rasputin was killed by a group of Russian nobles in 1916. The Tsarina happened to come from Germany and many Russians turned against her for being a German spy.

The February Revolution was mainly due to the suffering of the Russian people. Even if the army had won a few battles it is unlikely that this would have prevented people protesting.

Why is this both a good answer *and* a weak answer?

This answer makes five clear points and is balanced so would probably be given 9 marks. However, it contains unnecessary details and some irrelevant points – like the murder of Rasputin. This makes it a weak answer **because it is too long**. The extra time wasted on this answer would cut the amount of time available to get more marks in the other questions.

Marks given 9/9

Answer 2

Military defeats contributed to the outbreak of revolution in Russia in February 1917 but there were other factors such as food shortages in the cities, the suffering of the peasants and hatred for the Tsarina.

By February 1917, the Russian army had faced a series of bad defeats which damaged the morale of Russian soldiers and encouraged them to revolt against their leaders. The Tsar had taken control of the armed forces so he was blamed for the defeats and Russians wanted to get rid of him.

However, there were other reasons for the revolution. People in the cities faced severe shortages of food because so many peasants had gone to fight. The railway system was in chaos so fuel and other supplies were not reaching the cities. There were massive shortages in the countryside and peasants had had enough. Few Russians had any respect for the Tsarina who had been left to rule Russia but was accused of being a German spy.

Military defeats did affect the morale of the people but they had probably become used to hearing bad news from the front. It was the suffering of the people that pushed them into revolt in February 1917.

Why is this a good answer?

The answer contains at least five clear points which are carefully organized into points 'for' and points 'against' the importance of military defeats. The answer finishes with a conclusion which gives a supported answer to the question.

Marks given 9/9

Example

Question

Evaluate the usefulness of Source A as evidence about the reasons for the 1905 revolution. (5 marks)

Source A is part of a petition to the Tsar before the 1905 Revolution. (1905)

> We, the working men of St Petersburg, along with our wives, children and the old, pray that you will help us. We hope that you will be fair to us and protect us. We have become very poor – like beggars. Work has become too hard and we are very tired. We are no longer respected but are insulted by our treatment. We no longer feel like human beings but are being treated like slaves. We have hardly any food and are starving.

Answer 1

Source A is very useful as evidence about the reasons for the 1905 revolution. It tells us that working men of St Petersburg and their wives and children are praying for help. They are like beggars, working hard, feeling tired with hardly any food.

Why is this a weak answer?

The answer begins with a straight copy of the question so the marker is unsure whether the candidate has understood what the question is asking. The rest of the answer consists of bits of information taken from the source without answering the question. The last sentence is a list of bits of information separated by commas. You should always try to make each point in a separate sentence. There is no attempt to evaluate the source by considering who wrote it, why and when and what information is missing.

Marks given – this answer would be lucky to get 1/5

Answer 2

Source A provides useful evidence about the reasons for the 1905 Revolution because it comes from the actual petition carried by St Petersburg protesters. It is useful because it was written in 1905 immediately before the revolution broke out. It is useful because it was written to set out the problems being faced by Russian workers. It provides accurate detail because it mentions that the people are being treated like slaves and that they have hardly any food.

However the source is less useful because it doesn't describe the problems being faced by people living in the countryside. Nor does it mention that things were going badly in Russia's war with Japan which was another reason for the 1905 Revolution.

Why is this a good answer?

The answer makes at least five clear, relevant points from recall. Each of these points is explained or developed in a way that helps answer the question. Good use is made of facts and figures to support the points made.

Marks given 5/5

Chapter 18

Free at Last? Civil Rights in the USA, 1918–1968

Example

Question

Explain the reasons why many Americans supported immigration restrictions in the 1920s. (6 marks)

Answer 1

Many Americans supported immigration restrictions because they did not want black people coming to live in the South. The Ku Klux Klan claimed that black people were inferior to white people and had no right to live in the same areas as white people. They wanted black people to have separate schools, restrooms and lunch-counters.

Why is this a weak answer?

This answer includes a serious error. Immigration to America in the 1920s did not involve black people. Most black Americans were descended from people who had been taken from Africa hundreds of years earlier to work as slaves. If a question asks about the problems of immigration in the 1920s, don't write about African-Americans.

    Marks given 0/6

Answer 2

Many old immigrants wanted more restrictions placed on immigration because they were prejudiced towards the new immigrants whom they believed to be taking advantage of America's open door policy. Most old immigrants had come from Britain, Germany and Scandinavia and did not like the new immigrants who came from other countries. Many new immigrants came from Italy or Eastern Europe and it was assumed that they would speak no English. Many were Catholic, Orthodox or Jewish whereas most old immigrants believed Protestantism was the true religion of the USA. New immigrants were accused of taking jobs and homes from old immigrants. Also new immigrants were often accused of being heavily involved in violent crime.

Why is this a good answer?

The answer makes at least six clear, relevant points from recall. Each of these points is explained or developed in a way that helps answer the question.

    Marks given 6/6

Example

Question

Compare the views of Sources A and B about the success of the sit-ins. (4 marks)

Sources A and **B** describe the sit-ins.

Source A

Some civil rights workers believed that the sit-ins showed students that they could take action themselves. Young black people realised that they could make a difference to civil rights by winning the support of both black and white Americans. However, sit-ins only achieved limited success in some of the towns and cities where the protests were used. Much more needed to be done to improve civil rights.

Source B

The very act of protesting meant the students believed they could make a difference. When they 'sat in' these young people practiced non-violence, they dressed in their best clothes and they studied books. This helped to encourage black community support and won the respect and even admiration of some white Americans. However, the sit-ins only enjoyed success in a few southern states. In the Deep South, white Americans refused to desegregate and the protestors faced resistance from the white authorities.

Answer 1

Both sources say that the sit-ins showed that young students could take action themselves. Source A says that much more needed to be done but Source B doesn't mention this. Also Source B mentions that the students used non-violence but Source A doesn't tell us this.

Why is this a weak answer?

There is a simple comparison made in the first sentence which would get one mark. A comparison must be backed up with evidence from both sources in order to get two marks. The other two sentences do not contain comparisons. Avoid mentioning what a source doesn't tell us when comparing sources.

   Marks given 1/4

Answer 2

Sources A and B agree about the success of the sit-ins. Source A says that they showed students that they could take action themselves. Source B agrees with this by saying that the sit-ins showed students that they could make a difference. Source A points out that the sit-ins only achieved limited success in some towns and cities and Source B supports this saying that sit-ins only enjoyed success in a few southern states.

Why is this a good answer?

The answer starts by pointing out that the two sources agree. It then makes two clear points of comparison. Both the comparisons are backed up with evidence from each source.

   Marks given 4/4

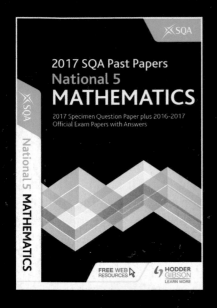
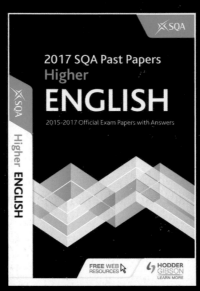